LAUGHTER THE

Laughter Therapy

How to Laugh About Everything in Your Life That Isn't Really Funny

ANNETTE GOODHEART, Ph.D.

LESS STRESS PRESS
SANTA BARBARA / 1994

Printed in the United States of America

ISBN 0-936941-05-7

Design and typography by Jim Cook

Published by Less Stress Press
Post Office Box 40297
Santa Barbara, California 93140-0297

To my mother, Helen,

who believed in laughter

To my daughter, Laura,

who believes in me

And to my granddaughters

Ellen, Alexandra, Olivia,

and Melissa,

who were born believing

and laughing

Contents

Introduction

> This life is a test—it is only a test. If it had been an actual life, you would have received further instructions on where to go and what to do.
>
> —*Anonymous*

I help people bring more laughter into their lives. At Santa Barbara City College I taught classes in laughter for ten years. I've traveled all over the United States, Japan, Canada, Australia, and Europe giving lectures, leading workshops, and training therapists, counselors, and health care professionals. I also work with businesses and corporations training employees how to use laughter to enhance enjoyment and creativity in their work. I'm fifty-nine now, and if you had told me twenty or thirty years ago that this is what I'd be doing, I would have said you were nuts. I thought of myself as a painter, a wife, and a mother.

I was born during the depression, the youngest of three children. My father was a math teacher, who I seldom saw because he had another job at night assembling irons in a factory. I remember him as hardworking, responsible, and very, very serious. On the other hand, my mother was always able to laugh readily. She was a physically fearless person, and I remember listening to her tales of physical feats as a fancy high diving champion. She was an artist and I was able to learn by watching her.

In spite of this, my childhood was isolated and lonely. I remember wandering down the block before the age of two, knocking on doors of neighbor ladies who would invite me in and feed me sweets. Unfortunately, it was during this time that I was sexually molested by two neighbor boys.

I am telling you this because often people ask me for my credentials for being a laughter therapist. I realize they often want to know that I have a B.A., two M.A.s, and a Ph.D. But I consider my real credentials to be the pain I have incurred in my lifetime. Because I am a laughter therapist, people often assume I had a happy childhood. However, the belief system I operate with as a laughter therapist is that all laughter comes out of pain - not that we laugh because we are happy.

I have been a compulsive overeater most of my life and relate it to my early experience of sexual abuse. (A high percentage of people with eating disorders have been sexually molested.) My life as a teenager was pure hell. I was overweight and had a complexion problem. Yet in high school I was cartoonist for the school newspaper. I would lurk in the dark recesses of the hallway when the newspaper came out to see if people were actually laughing at my cartoons. I finished high school in three years and at age sixteen I entered college, where my interest in cartooning continued. I cartooned for the humor magazine and the newspaper, and did almost all the posters and art projects for the campus. I had a wonderful time in college, but as a student, my grades were terrible. I was an art major and flunked many required courses in my own field of study. I had to take them over and barely received my degree.

I was married in the mid-fifties and had three children in short order. Marriage and motherhood, especially in those days, were very serious business. I married a man who abused alcohol and eventually became a full-blown alcoholic. I became a full-blown co-alcoholic. When we moved to Santa Barbara, I enrolled in the University of California's master of fine arts program, which was also very serious. My paintings became less fun and more arty. I started teaching art classes at the local city college as a student teacher. When the head of the department left due to illness, I stepped in on short notice to teach his art history classes. I was determined to make these courses interesting since I had flunked almost all of them.

This was the beginning of the end of seriousness. As a teacher I encouraged my students to call me by my first name and to get to know each other. I used unconventional means of transmitting information about art with great success. Projects included earthworks at the beach, happenings, packaging our classroom with paper and string (à la the artist Christo), and group paintings. The classes were fun, and the students and I enjoyed them immensely. I quit teaching when I was told point-blank that my position was going to be filled by a man and therefore I could not apply for it on a permanent basis. My marriage dissolved shortly afterward.

I had been in conventional therapy for three years in an attempt to salvage my marriage. It was a very serious kind of therapy, typical in that it was made up mostly of talk. I was also in a therapy group and became adept at being a group member and sharing what was going on with me. This was a new experience for me, as I had always channeled those needs through art.

Through a friend, I became involved in a peer counseling organization that focused on catharsis. In the first six weeks of my involvement with this group, I made more progress and changed my life more spectacularly than I had in my previous three years of conventional therapy. I spent my first year in catharsis laughing. The second year I relearned how to cry. I became a teacher and workshop leader and was a member of this organization for some years.

I developed a reputation as a laugher and as a peer-counselor with a light touch. Even though this organization was adamant about the power of catharsis, laughter was given minor lip service. The big thing was to cry.

After eight years of practicing therapy without a license, I decided to return to school, this time for a master's degree in psychology. While I was writing a paper about laughter and tears, someone referred me to Norman Cousins. They had seen him on television describing how he laughed himself through a life-threatening illness. His book had not yet been published, so I arranged to go and visit him at UCLA.

After our meeting, I realized that, although he had had a profound experience with laughter's healing properties, Cousins lacked a theoretical frame of reference about how laughter worked. Since I had been working with laughter as catharsis for eight years, I had already developed that frame of reference. I also knew that, because of his well-known name, Cousins would put laughter on the map. I made a conscious decision to go public with laughter.

When I returned to Santa Barbara I contacted the University of California and offered to do a laughter workshop. They laughed and signed me up. My first workshop was called Laugh Your Way to Health. Within a few months, I was teaching a second course, entitled Laughter for Living, through Santa Barbara City College Adult Education.

My Tuesday night laughter class quickly became one of the most popular classes in Adult Education. People would take the class over and over again, and many new people who wished to get in couldn't. As a result, I suggested an additional class, and thus was born Beginning Laughter and Advanced Laughter. It was in these classes that I practiced and refined my theories and presentations on the subject of laughter. I owe a debt of gratitude to the people of Santa Barbara who went through my laughter classes for ten years, allowing me to use them as guinea pigs.

I can pretty much say that, at the time, we were the only laughter class in the world. Since then, many other groups have sprung up, and a whole laughter program has been developed by the University of California at Santa Barbara. There have been many spin-offs from my class and my workshops. People have gone back to their own communities and instigated their own programs. When I train professionals, I give them a basic outline on how to teach laughter so that it will proliferate in a healing way.

I have decided to write a book because so many people have asked me if I have one. My experience has shown that there is a great deal of curiosity surrounding laughter, and an interest in relearning how to do it.

As a therapist, I've had thousands of hours of experience working with people suffering from minor ailments and terminal illnesses, including cancer, AIDS, MS, and arthritis; I have worked with anorexics, survivors of sexual abuse, and the suicidally depressed. The good news is that laughter is a powerful healing force. It's not a panacea, but it can be part of any program for healing—physically, emotionally, or spiritually.

The goal of this book is to empower one to bring more healing laughter into one's life and to become laughter independent. I encourage you to stay skeptical but open. My theory about laughter is probably different from what you grew up believing, but try it on for size. Then take what's useful to you and discard the rest.

There are many benefits you can reap from adding more laughter to your life. You can . . .

— Strengthen your immune system
— Make your cheeks sore
— Enhance your cardiovascular flexibility
— Embarrass your teenagers
— Increase your spirit quotient
— Think more clearly
— Put a devilish twinkle in your eye
— Increase your intellectual performance and information retention
— Forget what you were laughing about
— Replenish your creative juices
— Destroy your conservative reputation
— "Pop" yourself out of emotional ruts
— Dampen your undergarment
— Release and transform emotional pain
— Develop abdominal muscles of steel
— Rebalance the chemistry of your stress and tension
— Create stress and tension in others
— Create perspective and remind yourself of the bigger picture
— Wonder why you wasted all those years being serious
— Experience a deep connection with other human beings
— Confuse and confound family and friends
— Draw yourself into experiencing the present
— Help yourself live and die, laughing
— Join a growing group of giggling gurus

> This life is a test—it is only a test. If it had been an actual life, you would have received further instructions on where to go and what to do.
>
> —*Anonymous*

Acknowledgments

In order to be disciplined enough to write this book, I engaged the services of two wonderful women I came to refer to as my writer-sitters.

Robin Ferry, an accomplished dancer, was my first sitter. I want to thank her for listening to my moans and groans, my wailings and failings, and sharing her deep, rich laughter with me.

My second sitter was Janice Miglaccio, who in addition to being a published writer, turned out to be a great listener and an on-the-spot excellent editor.

I thank Cynthia Anderson for expertly editing the final draft.

My daughter, Laura Scully, not only proofread a disastrous early draft, but also proofed the book after publication, making numerous astute and gentle corrections and suggestions.

Jim Cook has been a delightful advisor on many graphic projects, including the design of this book. Thank you, Jim, for your cheerful patience and tasteful but zippy creativity.

I heap deep appreciation on all my clients who honored me by trustingly sharing their pains, hopes, laughter, and tears. They not only taught me many things, but they paid me as I learned!

Particularly I thank those who provided the client stories found in this book. Names and some facts have been changed to protect their confidentiality.

PART ONE

How to Laugh About Everything in Your Life That Isn't Really Funny

"From the moment I picked your book up
until I laid it down I was convulsed with laughter.
Someday I intend reading it."

—*Groucho Marx*

CHAPTER 1

The Big Tee-Hee

Earth laughs in flowers.

—*Ralph Waldo Emerson*

And Abraham was a hundred years old, when his son Isaac was born unto him. And Sarah said, God hath made me to laugh, so that all that hear will laugh with me.

—*Genesis 21: 5-7*

We are taught in this culture to face our problems straight on, to be brave, and to strive to solve those problems, not avoid them or skirt the issues. We all want to do the right thing, and so we try hard to solve our problems as our culture has taught us—head on, directly, and with great seriousness. This approach is often paralyzing. It is remarkable that we do as well as we do under these circumstances.

In observing children we notice that they play with their problems. They set up scenarios and, in a very creative way, they play with different possibilities. In adult terms, this kind of play is called creativity. Einstein said, "I play with ideas"—and he came up with some humdingers. What I am suggesting here is a different attitude toward our problems than we have experienced as products of our culture.

THE TEE-HEE EXPERIMENT

Laughter is the loaded latency given us by nature as part of our native equipment to break up the

> stalemates of our lives and urge us on to deeper and more complex forms of knowing.
>
> —*Jean Houston*

Let's try an experiment. Think of a problem in your life, something current that weighs you down, that feels like a burden, and that you would like to feel better about, perhaps even laugh about. You have just been notified that the IRS is going to audit your tax returns back to 1980. Your teenager, who has just learned how to drive, has had a fender bender with your brand new car. Or, at work, a younger, recently hired employee has been promoted to your level or above. These suggestions might trigger your own memory of a problem you need to solve in your life. Now, take that problem and pretend it is your right hand. Flatten your hand, keep your fingers together, and put your hand up to your face, the palm just touching the tip of your nose. This represents how we have been taught to handle our problems: to pay close attention and focus intently.

You will notice as you are holding your hand next to your face that your forward vision is drastically reduced. If you wanted to see straight ahead, it would be impossible. You can, however, with your hand in this position, still have peripheral vision and get bits of light through the cracks between your fingers. If you wanted to make any kind of forward movement you might very well stumble over some large object, but you could maneuver your way about just by the sight you have left. Because so much of your ability to see is blocked, it creates the sensation of isolation. Needless to say, no one would recommend that you walk through the world with your hand in front of your face.

What I want to suggest right now is that you keep that hand in front of your face, right at the nose, and if you are someone with an IRS audit coming up, just say to yourself, "The IRS—tee-hee." Immediately move your hand about a foot away from your nose. Just the suggestion of these two ideas together can be enough to shift your attitude. And moving your hand moves the problem far enough away so you can begin to see it in the context of the bigger picture. It is the same size problem, the same hand, but you have more vision; you can see better.

For those of you who actually laughed when you said "The IRS tee-hee," move your hand all the way out at arm's length. You will notice once again that your hand looks a good deal smaller than when it was up against your nose, or even a foot away from it. Suddenly, your problem has a context within its immediate environment, its world, its universe. This gives you remarkable perspective. It lets you know that your problem is not as big as you thought, that you are not isolated, and your vision is not blocked. When you have more vision, you have the opportunity to choose from a wider variety of alternatives and your choice is more appropriate in the bigger picture.

PLAYING WITH OUR PAIN

> Of course they are often sympathetic with me while they laugh! Playful pain—as you say—that is what humor is. The minute a thing is over-tragic it is funny.
>
> —*Charlie Chaplin*

The tee-hee experiment illustrates the basic skill of being able to laugh about all those things in our lives that aren't really funny, or, in simpler terms, to be able to play with our stress, our tension, and our pain—something that previously had been like a hand against the tip of our nose. Wise people have often said that it isn't what happens to us that is so difficult, but rather how we relate to what happens to us. To be able to laugh or even contemplate laughing about our problems is enough to shift our attitude. Once our attitude shifts, we think more clearly, we care more carefully, and we enjoy our lives more by connecting not only with ourselves and others, but also with our universe.

CALVIN'S HEAVY LEGACY

> Don't take life too seriously; you will never get out of it alive.
>
> —*Elbert Hubbard*

How on earth did we ever get into this serious framework—this incredibly heavy, ponderous, and burdensome way of viewing life? In searching for an answer to this question, I remained in somewhat of a dilemma until a surprising experience provided me with at least part of the answer.

Some years ago, I had several invitations to travel to Europe to do laughter work. So I organized a laughter tour of the continent. This took me from Italy through Switzerland and Belgium and up to Norway. Needless to say, I was very excited about this upcoming Laugh Tour. When I told people that I was going to Geneva for a week to do laughter work, they laughed, saying, "Nobody laughs in Switzerland." I was incredulous, believing that laughter is universal among human beings. It had never occurred to me that there were cultures that did not laugh.

I arrived in Geneva curious and apprehensive, and ready to observe whether what I had been told was true. Much to my horror and dismay, it was. As I traveled through the city, I noticed that children just out of school were not laughing. Nor were people laughing as they walked along the street talking to one another, or in restaurants and other circumstances. They were very well dressed, very prosperous looking, and very busy about their business. That evening, with great trepidation, I held my first laughter presentation. The turnout was very gratifying, considering my doubts as to whether anyone at all would show up. After making brief introductory remarks and laughing nervously a great deal, I was astounded at the response. People, following my cue, began to laugh so hard that they were literally rolling around on the floor, in their business suits, with tears pouring down their faces. A photographer from Illustre, the equivalent of our Life magazine, was laughing so hard as he rolled around on the floor that someone finally picked up his camera and snapped a picture of him. (Needless to say, it was not the picture they chose to publish!) I was amazed. I had never seen a group of people react so strongly and so quickly to my message.

When people came up for air, in my astonishment I began to ask questions.

"I was told you don't laugh here. What's going on?"

Someone burst out, "We've been waiting for you for three hundred years!"

Being the good little therapist that I am, I dutifully asked, "What happened three hundred years ago?"

They shouted, "John Calvin!" (whose home town just happened to be Geneva). He and his cohort, John Knox, had brought that culture a puritanical approach to life that is still reflected in the Swiss view of laughter.

Calvinism has played a tremendous part not only in the Swiss view of life, but in our own. As I reflected on this extraordinary response at the Geneva workshop, I realized that the Swiss had been waiting for someone to come along and remind them that they had permission to laugh. I will never forget that experience. It taught me the power of Calvinistic ideals. In America, that power has been transferred, through Puritanism and our early settlers, into a entire approach toward life, which has become ingrained and institutionalized throughout our culture.

LAUGHTER, EAST AND WEST

> How much lies in laughter—the cipher key,
> wherewith we decipher the whole man!
>
> —*Thomas Carlyle*

Probably one of the earliest statements encouraging the repression of laughter comes from Plato, who said, "Men of worth must not be represented [in comedy or literature] as overcome by laughter, and still less should we allow such a representation of the gods . . . we should not cultivate laughter lest some of what we are laughing at rubs off on us. In heavy laughter, too, we lose rational control of ourselves, and so become less than fully human."

Aristotle follows up with, "Too much laughter is incompatible with living the good life." (Conversely, Mae West said, "Too much of a good thing is wonderful!") With this kind of historical foundation, it is not surprising that Western culture has adopted such a serious approach to life.

While we may agree with John Calvin that control of our lives and consistent rationality are things to be desired, his extreme view (to the exclusion of anything hinting at joy) is evident in our current religious attitudes. John Calvin, of course, was a product of the Judeo-Christian tradition, which teaches that suffering will exonerate us from guilt, either real or imagined. Some years ago, Playboy magazine printed a drawing of Jesus laughing. They reported receiving more irate and upset letters as the result of that picture than of any other picture they had ever published.

In contrast, some Eastern philosophies place laughter next to enlightenment. This has produced the image of the laughing Buddha, along with many humorous Sufi and Zen stories. Zen Buddhists believe that if someone can laugh fifteen minutes after awakening in the morning, it is equivalent to six to eight hours of zazen (a form of rigorous meditation that requires the participant to sit on a stiff, black pillow and maintain his or her attention totally in the present). My sense of efficiency is gratified by achieving the same results in such a short amount of time with laughter.

The Eastern philosophies that regard laughter as sister to enlightenment provide for laughter in a very different way than we do. An example of this is Kochi, Japan, a town that devotes one full day to pure laughter and dancing. Anyone who does not participate is considered ignorant.

Compare Western and Eastern views of the creation of the universe. The Old Testament account is that God worked six days and rested the seventh. In contrast, Hindus view the creation of the universe as an act of play. Which of these two approaches appeals to you more?

WATTS' MIDDLE WAY

> In this ecstatic laughter he loses all memory, all desire, cries out to the immediate present of the world, and needs no other knowledge.
>
> —*Milan Kundera*

Probably the person most responsible for our current interest in Eastern philosophy is Alan Watts. After receiving a classical Oxford education, Watts became a Buddhist and came to California with a wonderful blend of knowledge and experience in both Eastern and Western religions. He gave many seminars and presentations at Esalen Institute and was very popular for his clear and astute philosophy, which blended these two diverse approaches into new ways of thinking about the world. He was famous for a very hearty and rich laugh. One of my favorite quotes is his reflection on the nature of the universe as "a system that creeps up on itself, says boo and laughs at itself for jumping, forgets that it did so before so it can do it again, and never becomes bored."

THE WEST IT IS A-CHANGING

> Coincidences are spiritual puns.
>
> —*G.K. Chesterton*
>
> Humor is a prelude to faith and
> Laughter is the beginning of prayer.
>
> —*Reinhold Niebuhr*

I hear many reports that Catholic churches are using more and more laughter in sermons and the confessional. Things seem to be changing. Even theological thinking about seriousness and laughter in Western culture has shifted somewhat. Thomas Merton, the greatly revered Trappist monk, was very aware of the importance of laughter and was famous for his sense of humor. When reflecting on the seriousness of religion, he said, "It certainly is a wonderful thing to wake up suddenly in the solitude of the woods and look up at the sky and see the utter nonsense of everything, including all the solemn stuff given out by professional asses about the spiritual life; and simply to burst out laughing and laugh and laugh with the sky and trees because God is not in words, and not in systems, and not in liturgical movements, and not in 'contemplation' with a big C, or asceticism or anything like that, not even in the apostolate, certainly not in books. I can go on writing them for all that, but one might as well make paper airplanes out of the whole lot."

If there is one thing that Eastern philosophy has brought to our attention, particularly Zen Buddhism, it is the notion of having our attention in the present and being in the here and now. One of the most extraordinary things about laughter is that it is impossible to laugh and not have one's awareness in the present. It is a totally present activity. It is impossible to laugh and think about what you need to get at the grocery store or pick up at the cleaners or what someone said to you earlier at the office. When we laugh, we are here, in the moment.

NOW IS ALL WE'VE GOT

> The difference between pain and suffering is the difference between what is and what you want it to be.
>
> —*Stephen Levine*

Several years ago I was asked to do a presentation for a group of physicians at a medical symposium on alternative approaches to chronic pain. I was one of the alternative approaches. After giving the information in lecture form, I asked for a volunteer to demonstrate how to work on chronic pain with laughter. A woman who came forward reported that she had arthritis in her hand and wrist and that moving it was difficult. She was in constant pain. After working with her for about ten minutes with laughter, she not only reported that the pain was gone, but she also demonstrated flexibility of movement.

I asked for any comments or questions from the audience. A psychiatrist raised his hand and said that what he saw me doing was hypnotizing her. After recovering from my surprise at his remark, I thought a while, and finally answered that his observation was understandable. "When we laugh, we are totally in the present," I said, "and in this day and age, the present appears to be an altered state." My response brought the house down.

If you walk down the main street of your city or town and observe people coming toward you, you will notice that most people are so preoccupied that they are unaware of their surroundings; they seem as if in a trance. We've all had the experience of greeting friends on the street and not being acknowledged until we shout our hello. They are so busy thinking, worrying, or daydreaming that they are "out of this world." They are operating on automatic pilot with their attention on something other than the present. This is one of the great tragedies of our time since the here and now is all we have—this is it! This is all we've got, this exact moment.

THE BIG TEE-HEE

> Perhaps the mission of those who love mankind is to make people laugh at the truth, to make truth laugh, because the only truth lies in learning to free ourselves from insane passion for the truth.
>
> —*Aristotle*

> Each instant represents a little universe, irrevocably forgotten in the next instant.
>
> —*Milan Kundera*

In its split-second simplicity, the present moment is meaningless. It is a unique adult requirement that life must have meaning. Babies do with life what was meant to be done—live it! By superimposing meaning onto life, we intellectualize it and distance ourselves from it. We watch from the sidelines, becoming bystanders, scholars, or voyeurs. Distanced from life, we become isolated, alienated, and serious.

Over the years, as I began to grasp this, I developed a personal philosophy about life that has supported me and helped me laugh. It is a very simple philosophy: If life is made up of one meaningless moment after another (one split second tacked on to the next), how do I respond to these moments? I decided that the only thing I can do with such moments is to enjoy them. I don't always succeed, but it is a wonderful goal. It makes me laugh when I tell people about it because it is so contrary to my own Puritan, Calvinistic upbringing, which taught me to be serious and look outward with great heaviness, putting tremendous weight and portent on everything I thought and did.

Writing this book has been a perfect example of that seriousness. Being a writer by neither training nor talent, I find that simply facing a blank page is seriousness personified. When I stare at that blank paper, I put great meaning onto the act of writing and getting my message across. Writing becomes very personal. When I am able to view the act of writing as a process of adding one word to the next, the task becomes lighter and more enjoyable. Sid Caesar once said, "Life isn't personal." This statement always forces me to examine how seriously I am reacting to my universe. Voltaire said that "God is like a comedian playing to an audience that is afraid to laugh." Maybe this whole thing is one gigantic cosmic joke! Maybe the universe wasn't created by a big bang, but perhaps by a big TEE-HEE!

> What if everything is an illusion and nothing exists? In that case, I definitely overpaid for my carpet.
>
> —*Woody Allen*

CHAPTER 2

Three Myths About Laughter that Keep Us From Laughing

> It is bad to suppress laughter. It goes back down and spreads to your hips.
>
> —*Fred Allen*

There are three myths about laughter that keep us from laughing as much as we need to or want. The first myth is that we must have a reason to laugh. The second is that we laugh because we are happy. The third is that a sense of humor is the same thing as laughter. I hope to dispel these myths and reveal to you what I believe to be the reality of laughter.

MY MINI LAUGH-A-THONS

> Laugh! Laugh! Laugh! Anybody who is any body will admire you and you'll confuse the rest.
>
> —*Kirsten Flagstad*

Every presentation and every workshop that I give I start by laughing. I stand in front of the group and laugh and laugh and laugh. On some occasions, I actually have laughed two or three minutes. If you have ever laughed for two or three minutes, you know how long a period of time that is for pure laughter.

I have been doing this since a remarkable experience I had at a conference in central California some years ago. I had been invited to do a series of laughter workshops for a religious retreat near Monterey. The workshops were to take place daily for an hour and a half, running concurrently with other workshops by other presenters. The opening night of the retreat was attended by all one thousand participants; each of the presenters was given one minute to sell his or her workshop to the attendees.

As the twenty or thirty presenters stood behind the curtain waiting to convince people of the superiority of their workshop over all others, the tension mounted. The person timing this event was militantly moving presenters on and off stage, and those of us left in line eyed each other with increasing covert competitiveness. I was experiencing this very strongly; in my desperation, my brain went totally blank.

As I stepped out into the bright lights before a thousand expectant faces, I began to laugh—something I often do in tense situations. As I laughed, I realized that perhaps it was all I needed to do, so I continued. Since I had been introduced by my name and the name of my workshop, the audience knew my topic. A wonderful man in the third row caught the laughter contagion. He and I keyed off one another and laughed for the full minute, as others joined in. I left the podium to the next tense and competitive presenter. My workshops burst their seams with participants.

That spontaneous laughter taught me something very important: In order to get across my message, I must be an example of what I present. Faced with a ludicrous task (a one-minute presentation of a week-long workshop), I found a way to thoroughly enjoy the process. My laughter relieved all the tension, stress, and pain that I had felt backstage. I practice what I preach.

THE LAUGHTER CONTAGION

> The most wasted day of all is that on which we have not laughed.
>
> —*Sebastian Roch Nicolas Champort*

I am aware, however, that when I begin my presentations this way, many people in the audience become extraordinarily uncomfortable. Some begin to whisper and talk, while others wait with very serious, concerned expressions on their faces, perhaps wondering if this person is a candidate for an institution. Some look very, very grim. The laughter seems to emphasize any heavy thoughts or feelings they brought with them. Fortunately, a portion of the group always joins in with the laughter, and we propel each other along. For whatever reason, this part of the group has not succumbed to those myths that prevent us from catching the contagion, which is innate to laughter.

MY LAUGHING BACKGROUND

> They love the Good; They worship Truth;
> They laugh uproariously in youth.
>
> —*Rupert Brooke*

The only time my family was ever together for any length of time, other than holiday occasions, was at dinnertime. My brother, my sister, my mother, and I would often sit around the dinner table for two to three hours laughing. (My father didn't laugh, but observed with amazement.) I think dinner went on long after we finished eating because everyone enjoyed the wonderful release, relaxation, and connection that the laughter brought us as a group. We were not a close family, but this extraordinary event that happened every evening was very connecting and very powerful.

My mother had been raised in a laughing family, and her mother had been raised in a laughing family, so she always told us how important laughter was. My brother was usually the instigator. We would laugh so hard that we would cry. We would laugh until we fell out of our chairs. We would wet our pants and spit out our food and laugh harder because we had done those things. Then we would end up laughing because we were laughing, having forgotten what had started us off in the first place. As the laughter subsided, we would clear the table, perhaps bring dessert or something more to drink, and then start up again.

My father, however, had not been raised in a laughing family. He would sit at the head of the table observing this bedlam with a quizzical, somewhat disbelieving, look on his face. We would keep checking to see if he had a smile yet, and occasionally there would be a slight twitch at the edge of his mouth as he got out one or two chuckles. Because of his upbringing, laughter was not an experience that came easily to him. Though he was trained as an engineer—whose goal in life was to answer the question "Why?"—he never once asked us, "Why are you laughing?" I think intuitively he knew that something important was going on, and so he resisted stopping the laughter by asking why.

MYTH #1: YOU NEED A REASON TO LAUGH

> I am neither of a melancholy nor a cynical disposition, and am as willing and as apt to be pleased as anybody; but I am sure that, since I have had the full use of my reason, nobody has ever heard me laugh.
>
> —*Earl of Chesterfield*

The first major myth about laughter that prevents us from laughing as much as we need to is that we must have a reason to laugh. The people who respond to my opening laughter with great seriousness at my workshops may feel that there is no reason for me to be laughing, or if there is, they missed it. Not only must we have a reason to laugh, but the reason must be so good that when someone challenges us with "Why are you laughing? What's so funny?" when we explain it, they too will laugh. If they don't, very often we are presented with a puzzled face and a remark, such as, "That was it? Boy, do you have a weird sense of humor!"

Many of us unconsciously censor our laughter because at some level we think our reason for laughing is not good enough. It is important to note here that the reality is that laughter is unreasonable, illogical, and irrational. I propose that we don't need a reason to laugh. When we see a six-month-old baby laughing, we don't demand "What's so funny?" but rather delight in the response and often join in. We can do so with adults. Insisting on a reason to laugh is an excellent way of stopping someone, or ourselves, from laughing. All we have to do is ask "why?" When we begin to think, instead of respond, we stop laughing. This is very important to remember when we are in situations where laughter is inappropriate. We may want to ask ourselves, "Why am I laughing right now?" so that we can stop—for instance, if you get the giggles when pulled over by a policeman for speeding or some other infraction of the law.

MYTH #2: WE LAUGH BECAUSE WE ARE HAPPY

> I'm a cheerful woman, not a happy one—A happy woman has no cares—a cheerful one has cares, but has learned to laugh about them.
>
> —*Beverly Sills*

The second major myth about laughter is that we laugh because we are happy, when the reality is we're happy because we laugh. I ask my groups how many feel better after they have laughed, and there is always a unanimous show of hands. At this point I remark that if laughter came out of happiness, we wouldn't feel better after laughing—we would have already felt better before laughing.

> True happiness is of a retired nature and an enemy to pomp and noise; it arises in the first place from the enjoyment of one's self; and in the next from the friendship and conversation of afew select companions.
>
> —*Joseph Addison*

> Happiness is no laughing matter.
>
> —*Richard Whately, Archbishop of Dublin*

I think that laughter has been assigned the job of indicating happiness because we have been so desperate for some outward sign of this vague, undefined, but treasured state. Actually, most people (I am certainly one of them) don't know what happiness is. We know that the Declaration of Independence directs us to pursue it, but judging by our national behavior, we are somewhat confused about where happiness lies. If we feel better after we laugh, then laughter must come from a source other than happiness.

> Laughs are exactly as honorable as tears. Laughter and tears are both responses to frustration and exhaustion, to the futility of thinking and striving anymore. I myself prefer to laugh, since there is less cleaning up to do afterward—and since I can start thinking and striving again that much sooner.
>
> —*Kurt Vonnegut, Jr.*

Those of us who have laughed until we've cried know that in the middle of the process, we can't tell which is which. We do not laugh because we're happy and cry because we're sad—we laugh or cry because we have tension, stress, or pain. Laughter and tears re-balance the chemicals our bodies create when these distressed states are present, and so we feel better after we have laughed or cried.

> I laugh because I must not cry—
> that's all, that's all.
>
> —*Abraham Lincoln*

Many of us will not laugh because we believe that it indicates we are happy when we know we are not. Those people who attend my presentations feeling tired, sad, or frustrated find it difficult to respond to my laughter. If people are not feeling happy and they see some strange woman standing on a stage laughing, they can find no resource in themselves to join in, because obviously they are not happy and should not laugh. But my experience indicates that, if we can join in the contagion of laughter when we feel stress, tension, or pain, often we can experience the state we call happiness.

> We look before and after,
> And pine for what is not;

> Our sincerest laughter
> With some pain is fraught;
> Our sweetest songs are those that tell of saddest thought.
>
> —*Percy Bysshe Shelley*

MYTH #3: A SENSE OF HUMOR AND LAUGHTER ARE ONE AND THE SAME

> If I get big laughs, I'm a comedian. If I get little laughs, I'm a humorist. If I get no laughs, I'm a singer.
>
> —*George Burns*

The third myth is that a sense of humor is the same thing as laughter. I suggest that even though the two terms are used interchangeably, they are very different processes. The reality is that you don't need a sense of humor to laugh. When we see a six month old baby laughing, we don't remark, "Doesn't that baby have a wonderful sense of humor!" A sense of humor is learned, laughter is innate. A sense of humor is an intellectual process, whereas laughter spontaneously engages every major system in the body.

> A sense of humor is one thing no one will admit to not having.
>
> —*Mark Twain*

A sense of humor does not guarantee laughter in the person to whom we give that designation. Many people with great senses of humor don't laugh. Groucho Marx was known to have laughed only once, publicly or privately. Very often people who make other people laugh do so because they can control when the laughter will occur. The emphasis on humor diverts us from the broad scope of laughter that is available, making laughter a specialty which is then possible only occasionally.

> Humor . . . is essentially a complete mystery.
>
> —*E.B. White*

There is absolutely no agreement on what a sense of humor is or what makes something funny. Senses of humor vary according to culture, age, ethnic or economic background, race, sex, etc. I remarked to one of my groups that women in the ladies' room laugh at different things than men in the men's room. A man raised his hand and said, "Men don't laugh in the men's room." I didn't realize this, having spent very little time in the men's room. (Later on, a man came up to me and said he knew why men didn't laugh in the men's room . . . it is hard to laugh and aim at the same time!)

LAUGHTER IS NO LAUGHING MATTER

> Analyzing humor is like dissecting a frog. Few people are interested and the frog dies of it.
>
> —*E.B. White*

> Defining and analyzing humor is a pastime of humorless people.
>
> —*Robert Benchley*

In 1987, I attended the International Humor Conference in Arizona. For several days, scholars from all over the world read papers analyzing what makes people laugh. It was the most serious conference that I ever attended. No one was laughing but me, and I was desperately trying not to! It was so ironic to be at this serious humor conference that for me it was much like trying not to laugh in church.

THE WIDE WORLD OF LAUGHTER

> Genuine laughing is the vent of the soul, the nostrils of the heart, and it is just as necessary for health and happiness as spring water is for a trout.
>
> —*Josh Billings*

Laughter is universal, and the ability to laugh is common to all human beings. You can laugh with anybody or anything anywhere in the world, even if you don't share the same sense of humor. Laughter is innate, and it is also present in other species. Although I have never done it, I understand you can laugh with chimpanzees and gorillas, and I suspect that dolphins laugh. Dolphins seem to wear a perpetual smile and a twinkle in their eye, and when they pop out of the water and make that rhythmic, high-pitched noise, to me it sounds like laughter.

THE WHALES' TALE

Seven days without laughter makes one weak.

—*Joel Goodman*

Some years ago, I spent a week in Magdelena Bay, Baja California, the southernmost breeding ground of the California gray whale. I was there to be with the Paul Winter Consort and play flute with the whales. (Paul Winter and his musicians are famous for weaving jazz around sounds of various animals, particularly the humpback whale.) Twice a day, we would pile into skiffs and very quietly approach the whales and their calves as they rested on the surface of the water. We usually could get within twenty-five or thirty feet of them, but then they would dive and disappear.

After five days of sneaking up on these whales only to have them disappear from sight, the last hard-core whale watchers piled into the skiffs late in the afternoon to attempt one last close encounter. Luck was with us, and we came within about ten feet of a mother and her calf sleeping on the surface, almost touching her before she sounded. We were all so elated that we began to scream and laugh and clap and holler and release the mass of tension that had been built up all week, sneaking up on these leviathans again and again.

At that moment, something astounding happened. The whales began to come toward us. In fact, they began to splash and dive and roll over and flip their tails around and spy hop, a maneuver where the whale's head pops up in order to "spy." We had at least five whales putting on an unbelievable show of aquabatics. We sat in the boat observing in total disbelief.

When I got back to the main ship, I realized that if I were a whale being sneaked up on, I would want to get away too. But when this skiffload of humans began to lose control by laughing, shouting, hollering, and delighting in their world, I too would have felt more attracted to them, and would have wanted to express my delight and joy. I really believe that this is what occurred in the Baja breeding grounds between a small group of avid whale watchers and five joyful, jumping tons of whale.

LAUGHTER AND CONTROL

> [Laughter] moveth much aire in the breast, and sendeth the warmer spirits outward.
>
> —*Richard Mulcaster*

Animals are less frightened of us when we are not trying to control them or their environment. I think this encounter with the whales was an act of interspecies connection. When we acted freely as ourselves, they could act as themselves, and we could delight in one another.

Let's reflect back on the people in my audiences who witness my laugh-a-thon and begin talking to each other. By talking, they can avoid the loss of control that is natural to laughter. When we laugh, we literally lose physical control, and the loss of any control is a scary proposition for most humans. Because of laughter's natural contagion, if I am afraid of losing control, I will stop you from laughing. Or, if I am afraid of crying (because we all know that if we laugh hard enough, we will cry), I will try to control others' laughter.

> If you have no tragedy, you have no comedy. Crying and laughing are the same emotion. If you laugh too hard, you cry. And vice versa.
>
> —*Sid Caesar*

This book is about laughter, not about how to control or "make" others laugh. It is about helping ourselves laugh . . . laughing for no reason, laughing when we are not happy, and laughing when nothing is "funny." The paradox is that by losing control through laughter, we gain control of our lives in flexible, intelligent, creative, and caring ways and have a whale of a good time.

CHAPTER 3

The Dark Side of Laughter: Jokes, Teasing & Tickling

> I love such mirth as does not make friends ashamed to look upon one another next morning.
>
> —*Isaak Walton*

> Ridicule is just one phase of humor and is not always the basis for a laugh, although it's a surefire short cut. In ridicule, too, all those who laugh are not necessarily amused. Sympathy may be aroused for the poor fellow who is the object of ridicule.
>
> —*Mae West*

Laughter can be beneficial to our well-being because it heals and connects. It offers a universal form of communication that dissolves all barriers of language, age, nationality, race, and creed. When people laugh together, they feel closer.

However, laughter can be a weapon. In our desperation to find ways to laugh and thus relieve our tension, we often don't distinguish between laughter that heals and laughter that hurts. Some of the most common vehicles we use to stimulate laughter—jokes and teasing—have tremendous power to injure others because they are based on ridicule. Tickling, too, can be very destructive, because usually it is based on one person overpowering another—such as a parent cornering and tickling their child.

Laughter isn't always the best medicine. According to James Carroll of Central Michigan University, humor that has a "put-down component or humor that [shows] little compassion or empathy" is related to health problems. In a study of 79 college students, Carroll tried to link the students' states of health with their senses of humor. He found that the healthier a man is, the more sophisticated and "dry" his sense of humor tends to be. In women Carroll linked good health to "a flirtatious, playful" humor, a no-nonsense approach to sham and sentimentality, and a "scorn for male foolishness or ineffectuality." Unhealthy men liked humor that displayed a "hostile defiance against authority" and a "passive resignation to problems, particularly interpersonal problems with females."

SOME THOUGHTS ON RIDICULE AND CONFORMITY

> Everything is funny as long as it is happening to somebody else.
>
> —*Will Rogers*

> The real wit tells jokes to make others feel superior, while the half-wit tells them to make others feel small.
>
> —*Elmer Wheeler*

Webster defines ridicule as "the act or practice of inciting laughter at a person or thing by means of jesting words, caricature, mocking, etc.; slightly contemptuous banter."

During my seminars, I have noticed that occasionally someone will leave after five minutes. I've learned that people who have been ridiculed severely in childhood often feel that laughter of any kind is aimed directly at them, and they cannot tolerate laughter, even their own. This is a pathological state that stems from a constant barrage of ridiculing jokes and teasing from parents, peers, and siblings.

Laughter that stems from ridicule does not make us feel better about ourselves or others. If ridicule brought us closer together, we would have no racism, sexism, classism, ageism, heterosexism, etc. Ray Moody, a psychiatrist and author of *Laugh after Laugh,* said, "Ridicule is one of society's ways of preserving the status quo." It's only through the threat of ridicule that conformity becomes an essential part of our lives. The fear of being laughed at and therefore cast out is so great that we dare not deviate too far from what our particular group finds acceptable.

There were some Native American tribes that did not use physical punishment to discipline their children; they found ridicule a much more powerful and effective tool. Because we all sense at some level that our survival is based on our interdependence, the possibility of alienation or separation from the group is so threatening that we will do almost anything to avoid it—including ridiculing somebody else.

LAUGH NOW, PAY LATER: JOKES THAT HURT

> A jest's prosperity lies in the ear of him that hears it, never in the tongue of him that makes it.
>
> —*William Shakespeare*

There is an unwritten rule that we must be able to laugh at ourselves. We hear this most frequently when we protest a put-down joke, particularly when it is about a group with which we are associated. Stereotypical jokes, which put down groups of people, have three purposes. The first purpose is to support our prejudices by drawing others into agreement through laughter. It would then follow that the second purpose is to make the joke teller feel good: if he is the instigator of the laughter, then he feels good about himself in spite of the joke's hateful message. The third purpose is to reinforce the stereotype so that there is no threat to the status quo.

There is a presumption amongst joke tellers that we are born with a sense of humor (exactly like theirs), and that the resulting laughter will change our attitude about how seriously we take our situation. When we presume that we are born with a sense of humor, we get in trouble. Humor that involves these kinds of jokes does produce laughter, but probably from fear and anger.

This reinforces the attitude of the joke, and creates or reinforces stereotypes.

We are not born with a sense of humor, but we are born laughers. Laughter changes our attitudes and our perspective, and from that we can develop a sense of humor, or a way of viewing the world playfully. This approach allows our sense of humor to be inclusive of all people and not dependent on a specific joke or topic. An inclusive sense of humor is warm and connected, broad and universal. It allows us to play with situations that are stressful instead of playing with others' pain to create laughter.

A DEADLY DUO: JOKES AND GOSSIP

> She likes herself, yet others hates
> For that which in herself she prizes;
> And while she laughs at them, forgets
> She is the thing that she despises.
>
> —*Amoret*

I was asked to present a workshop on laughing and crying to the communications division of a police department in a major city. A lieutenant described the situation to me: "We're the people you call if you're getting assaulted, robbed, or murdered. Any time we pick up the phone a crime may be in progress. The tension that builds up, working that close to life and death, is tremendous."

The captain of this division told me his employees' problems included absenteeism, stomach problems, colds, headaches, alcohol and drug abuse, and high turnover—but he believed the number-one problem was internal: gossip. I learned that the personal communication between these professional communicators consisted, in large part, of ridicule. The officers and their helpers were teasing and telling jokes on each other—ethnic, racist, sexist, and ageist jokes. In a desperate attempt to relieve the stress of their jobs, they had reverted to the most common way of obtaining laughter—ridicule. Unfortunately, the ridicule was creating more stress. When I suggested that this type of humor was part of the problem, one officer responded sarcastically, "If you were a cop, you would understand."

All personnel were required to attend my workshop (two shifts of 250 people each day). I began by asking, "How many of you would rather be somewhere else?" Nearly all of them raised their hands. I picked out one officer near the front and asked him, "Where would you rather be?"

"At the beach!" he declared, and there was a chorus of laughing agreement.

"How about you?" I asked another one.

"At home," she said, "in bed." And again there were cheers.

I kept asking around the room, and each answer brought a more boisterous response and laughter. Everyone was laughing at their common plight, laughing with each other instead of at each other. Once they were loosened up, I even got them to chant in unison, first one side of the room and then the other: "WHAT ON EARTH AM I DOING HERE?"

The room was in an uproar of laughter and the feeling of resentment was defused. They were able to say what was actually on their minds. I told them I suspected it was difficult to be a police officer; to witness human degradation without becoming hardened; to be mistrusted by citizens and criminals alike; to be caught between policy and intuition; to be subjected to review board discipline for the slightest mistake in judgment.

I wanted them to see, and to appreciate, the pleasures and benefits of their work. Obviously there had to be some, or they'd be pursuing other occupations. I asked them to share with me what they liked about working at the police department. There was some hesitation at first. Finally, one man volunteered, "I like the job security." Another said, "I like the professionalism." Another said, "The early retirement. The pension." Another: "I like the status, the feeling I get when I put on my uniform in the morning." Another offered, "I like the excitement," and one woman said, "I like the responsibility." Some told stories about their favorite phone calls, the times when they'd talked people out of suicide, settled a family dispute, or helped an old woman to feel a little less lonely. One officer shared how good he felt when he was able to comfort a child after a devastating car accident. All of their vision and idealism came out.

It went on for a full hour, until a sergeant said, "You know, I've been with this division for eight years, and this is the first time I've heard anybody admit that they like working here!" There was spontaneous applause.

I took this opportunity to explain the difference between the good feelings they were sharing here, and the more destructive forms of interaction that went on daily within the division: jokes and teasing. Some were upset to hear this; they didn't want to give up jokes. Remembering what the captain had told me, I asked the group if anyone saw the connection between jokes and gossip.

A woman said, "It goes like this. If I'm working the boards and it's time to take a coffee break, I'll go have coffee with somebody. I might have a lot on my mind—I broke up with my boyfriend or I'm just feeling lousy that day—but I'm not going to talk about myself because that other person may use it for ammunition or make some wisecrack about it, to get laughs. So I'm going to keep quiet about myself. All we have to talk about is other people. You know—gossip!"

She had it exactly. When we try to let go of our stress through laughter obtained by ridiculing other people, we know we may end up as targets of ridicule. In this way the members of the communications division were causing even more stress between themselves than was coming at them from the violent outside world. They were creating a nontrusting, emotionally unsafe environment, one in which they spent eight stressful hours of their lives every day.

In order to begin addressing this situation, I made two suggestions to the group.

First, they were to agree to go one whole day without gossiping. In other words, if Sergeant Smith talked to Sergeant Jones in a nonprofessional capacity, they could talk only about themselves or each other. Talking about absent third parties would not be allowed.

Second, I wanted them to start sharing their embarrassing moments, to aim their laughter, not at others, but at their own misadventures. I asked them to use these stories to produce the laughter that has the power of connection, rather than alienation.

Without much prompting they began telling embarrassing stories about themselves on the job. One story would prompt another, and the laughter began to roll. They seemed to be getting the hang of it.

This workshop experience taught that there is a connection between gossip and ridicule and that, in a safe setting, people will gladly move from ridicule to more connecting laughter. I came away with a new appreciation for police officers.

LAUGHING AT YOURSELF CAN BE DANGEROUS TO YOUR HEALTH

> You can't hold a man down without staying down with him.
>
> —*Booker T. Washington*

> All of us have schnozzles—are ridiculous in one way or another, if not in our faces, then in our characters, minds or habits. When we admit our schnozzles, instead of defending them, we begin to laugh, and the world laughs with us.
>
> —*Jimmy Durante*

When I was introduced at a conference to another speaker as a laughter expert, he immediately offered to tell me a joke. When I objected, he insisted that it was an especially good joke. "Well," I asked, "does it have to do with a specific group of people?"

He admitted it was a Jewish joke, so I asked him to omit the reference to Jews.

"But it wouldn't be funny then," he protested.

"I don't listen to jokes that stereotype groups of people," I explained.

"But I'm a rabbi!" he exclaimed with great fervor.

•

"Laugh at yourself first before anyone else can," said Elsa Maxwell.

Very often, we excuse someone who tells a deprecating joke about their own group because they are merely laughing at themselves or, in this case, a group they belong to. This somehow gives them license to put down themselves and their own group. When people say, "Well, laughing at ourselves is very important," I agree that indeed it is, as long as we don't ridicule ourselves in the process. Laughing at our own group often serves as a way of keeping the group separate and cohesive in order to protect itself. Very often we put down our own groups in the same way outside groups do, thus perpetuating the racism, sexism, or whateverism that is coming from the outside. This undermines our group self-image so that we cling to each other in fear.

At one of my workshops, a man with an obviously Polish name introduced himself and immediately told a Polish joke. The group laughed. Sometimes someone in a wheelchair will make self-deprecating jokes, and, once again, the group will laugh. I challenged a man who did this. He said that it defused the tension most people feel around the disabled. By telling a joke on himself first, the power was in his hands and he could avoid feeling victimized by others. We who are able-bodied are so desperate for relief of our tension with the physically different, that we welcome any sort of laughter, even if it makes fun of the teller.

I often see this use of laughter among people who joke about their baldness, their weight, their height, or their age in a very put-down sort of way, thus keeping control and diffusing any real or imagined tension with laughter. However, it is possible to laugh at ourselves without self-deprecation or self put-down. We can merely relate the facts of our experience or situation without any judgment or criticism. The best example of this approach is sharing embarrassing moments. This is a very healthy and connecting process for us to share with others. (See Part II, #3, Share Your Embarrassing Moments.)

HANDLING JOKESTERS

> It dawned on me then that as long as I could laugh, I was safe from the world; and I have learned since that laughter keeps me safe from myself, too.
>
> —*Jimmy Durante*

People have developed many ways to deflect the jokes of chronic joke tellers. Nearly everyone has someone they care about who falls into this category. It is important for people to realize that chronic joke tellers need to be in control of the attention they receive and need to feel powerful by "making" someone laugh. These people have difficulty relating closely to others and need to hear from us that we love them in spite of the fact that they are "funny." It is also important not to laugh at their jokes, so they get our message.

Because I am fairly well known in my home town, people often approach me in public with "Aren't you the laugh lady?" When I respond they pounce on me with "Want to hear a funny joke?"

My face lights up and I respond with a delightful "NO!"

They always laugh. They then inquire, "Why not?"

"Because I don't listen to jokes," I say.

"Well, what do you laugh about then?"

"Everything! What's not to laugh about?"

THE ULTIMATE MANIPULATION: TEASING

> Like a madman who throws firebrands, arrows
> and death, is the man who deceives his neighbor
> and says "I am only joking!"
>
> —*Proverbs 26: 18-19*

I define teasing as using, without permission, inside information about how someone feels; in other words, emotional manipulation. The key word here is permission. Just as there is a small percentage of non-ridiculing jokes, there is a small percentage of non-hurtful teasing. However, most teasing is done without permission.

Teasing is another way of attempting to control other people and situations. When we tease someone, we expect them to be a good sport (laugh) when we are misusing inside information about them. This is a form of emotional abuse.

Teasing plays with another's pain, attempting to get the "teasee" to react so the teaser can laugh. If the person being teased objects and says, "You're hurting my feelings," that person will most likely be accused of being too sensitive. The teaser will say, "I was only teasing! Can't you take a joke?" This adds insult to injury.

Most of us have been teased as children, and as a result, we tease each other. Very few of us have taken the time to think about what teasing does, where it comes from, or what it is. I believe teasing revolves around issues of powerlessness, embarrassment, hostility, and anger.

THE CYCLE OF TEASING AND ANGER: THE STORY OF MICHAEL

Where there's laughter . . . there's hope.

—*Comic Relief, 1990*

A fourteen-year-old boy was brought in to see me by his parents. He was an attractive, gawky boy in that stage where he couldn't decide whether to be soft or tough. The family consisted of Michael, his father Randy, his twenty-six-year-old stepmother Deborah, and Randy and Deborah's girls, Tina, four, and Amy, three.

At the first session his stepmother complained that Michael teased his half-sisters "mercilessly." The boy squirmed when he heard this. I asked him: "Is this true? Do you tease the little girls?"

"Well, maybe it's true," he said reluctantly. "But they bug me all the time!"

Deborah tried to break in and defend her daughters on the basis of their tender ages. I wanted Michael to feel free to speak out about his feelings, so I prompted: "I'll bet those girls really know how to get you."

He rolled his eyes in dramatic agreement.

"It must really get to you," I said. "Here they are, only three and four years old, and they can outsmart you!"

He laughed tentatively at this suggestion, fidgeting around in the chair.

I asked him, "Well, doesn't it make you angry when the girls do that?"

"Yes," he said quietly.

"What do you do when you're angry?"

He shrugged his shoulders.

"Do you tease them back when you're angry?" I suggested.

He thought about it. "I guess so."

"You tease them to get even?"

He nodded his head quickly, glancing at his parents.

"But there's only one thing wrong," I told him, "and that's that it doesn't work, does it? They keep doing it, don't they?"

He thought about it. "Yeah," he said, somewhat enlightened.

I handed him a pillow from the couch. "Here," I said, pretend that this pillow is—which one, Tina or Amy?"

Michael squirmed again and laughed.

"Which one of them bugs you the most?" I asked.

"Tina," he said.

"Okay, that pillow is Tina. She has just done something to really bug you, and I want you to hit her."

Michael looked over at his parents to see if this was okay, and again he laughed tentatively. He was supposed to love his little half-sisters, not punch them out. He turned to the pillow and punched it lightly.

"Aren't you really mad at her?" I wondered. "Don't you want to hit her harder?"

He socked the pillow harder, and laughed.

"She's still twitching," I remarked.

He repeatedly slammed his fist into the pillow, laughing louder with each blow. No longer was he looking toward his parents for permission. I egged him on: "She's such a sweet little girl, never does anything bad, never gets punished."

Michael threw the pillow to the floor and stomped on it, laughing more and more and more. The parents watched in amazement, obviously disturbed to see the intensity of Michael's anger. Michael's parents mistook his anger for his true intentions, while the boy himself understood that he was taking care of his need to release anger through laughter.

When he finished attacking the pillow, Michael slumped back into his chair. Then he put his face in his hands and burst into tears. He sobbed deeply for a minute or so. He wiped away the tears, still sniffling, while his parents sat across the room, not knowing what to expect next.

Quietly, I asked him, "Michael? Do you know what you were crying about?"

"Yes," he said, "now I won't have to shoot darts at the sparrows."

I continued to see Michael, Randy, and Deborah separately and as a family. I stressed the importance to all three of Michael's need to release his anger appropriately, with a pillow in his room.

When I saw Michael alone, he would often decide to ignore me. He would slump back in the chair, put his head on the pillow, and pretend to be asleep. It was a good game, and I played along. I patted his head and sang him a lullaby. Pretty soon, his shoulders would begin to twitch. He was laughing. By sharing this game of laughter as a therapist I was able to keep the wheels of laughter greased. This facilitated his ability to laugh at home and release his anger appropriately, instead of teasing his sisters and killing sparrows.

"I LIKE YOU, I DON'T LIKE YOU": TEASING'S MIXED MESSAGE

> Jests that slap the face are not good jests.
>
> —*Cervantes*

Teasing is a mixed message. When teased, we are uncertain whether the teaser is trying to make affectionate contact with us in some strange way, or whether the teaser is actually expressing hostility. If we are angry with someone, we need to express it directly: "I am very angry." If we feel affectionate toward someone, it's most effective to say, "I like you." But to tease is to say neither and both.

I have observed that teasing is particularly prevalent among men. In our culture, men are taught to hide their feelings. It's not permissible for one man to say to another, "I like you." As a result, men tease each other in hopes that it will come across as caring. Unfortunately, teasing usually creates more tension because it is unclear communication.

TEASING OUR CHILDREN: A PAINFUL LEGACY

> Keep away from the wisdom that does not cry, the philosophy that does not laugh and the greatness that does not bow before children.
>
> —*Kahlil Gibran*

Teasing and laughing at our children begins very early. Certainly it is well placed by the time they start walking. How often have we watched our babies as they tentatively take their first steps and fall on their fannies with a thump. We laugh—they don't. This is such a common occurrence that we don't even think about it.

Then, when our babies start talking, their mispronouncing or mispositioning of words can be so incongruous that we tease them and laugh—but imagine what it must be like for them, not understanding why their parents are laughing. This view of children as sources of entertainment for adults is so common that even among very educated people, children are ridiculed in this manner.

Some brilliant friends of mine who were Ph.D.s in their respective fields had a three-year-old son. When people came over, they would ask their son to say his words. He would pronounce very large, complicated words with a very serious, intent look on his face to the great amusement of his audience, who would laugh and laugh and laugh as he continued to do what his parents asked. Little children are so desperate to please their parents by performing, that we as adults have taken undue advantage, using them to satisfy our need for laughter.

TEASING IS A POOR TEACHER ABOUT SEXUALITY AND RELATIONSHIPS

I have seen mothers in the park teasing their small children aged three or four because they are hugging, touching, or kissing a child of the opposite sex. Very often the mothers will say in a sing-song voice, "Johnny has a girlfriend, Johnny has a girlfriend," and laugh. The mothers' own tension and stress concerning relationships with men finds an unhealthy outlet by being projected onto their children.

Parents often tell their children that teasing by their peers is a sign of affection, when in reality it is physical or emotional abuse. When Suzie comes home from kindergarten and tells her mother that Johnny keeps pulling her hair, her mother may respond by saying, "That's because he likes you, dear." This kind of misinformation leads people into relationships that hurt. In extreme situations, it could lead to physically abusive relationships. The message is "When someone likes you, they hurt you. When someone loves you, it really hurts." The reality is love never hurts! But our actions and behaviors around love can hurt, especially teasing.

When our children reach puberty, all the pain and anguish we went through once comes again to the surface. Many women walk with caved-in chests because they were teased so brutally about developing breasts. Many men were teased about developing beards and changing voices. Unfortunately, as adults we often tease our children in the same way we were teased, perpetuating the cycle of embarrassment, humiliation, and shame.

Teasing our children does not promote their self-confidence. It is not surprising that as adults we have so many sexual hangups and so much difficulty in establishing healthy intimate relationships. The legacy of any teasing we experienced as children around sexuality and relationships can be extremely difficult to overcome.

When "America's Funniest Home Videos" became the highest rated series on TV, Entertainment Weekly reported what viewers found most amusing:

—A child getting hit with a shovel.
—A child falling from a swing.
—A man falling out of a boat.
—A child falling down a hill.
—Seven women falling off a bench.
—A man being hit by a glider.
—Another man being hit by a glider.
—A woman falling off a camel.
—A child bicycling into a tree.
—A child bicycling into a bush.

The top prize was awarded to a woman who had been thrown off a horse.

TECHNIQUES FOR HANDLING TEASING

How can we handle teasing when it is aimed at us? Several suggestions have come out of my groups, and I have tried some that work fairly well. The first is the straightforward approach. When someone is teasing me, I will say, "That hurts my feelings. I wish you wouldn't do that." I go on to explain that if they really want to be close to me and want me to share how I feel, I must have their agreement that they won't tease me. If they continue to tease me, I say, "I told you how your teasing hurts me and yet you continue to tease. Why do you want to hurt my feelings?"

Another way to interrupt teasing is to rephrase it. When someone is teasing me, instead of reacting in an angry way or expressing my hurt feelings, I will just say, "What I really hear you saying is that you like me." When the affectionate part of the teasing is made explicit, it results in laughter, thus lightening up a potentially unpleasant situation.

Finally, if you have a teasing relationship with someone, it is important that it be with mutual permission. Sometimes even asking is not enough, because a person who has been raised in a teasing environment may believe they have no right to object. It may be necessary to ask permission more than once. If the "teasee" feels free to tell you that you have gone too far with the teasing, then it is obvious that some teasing is permissible. When people tease each other with permission, they can laugh together in shared recognition of their shortcomings.

No child gives an adult permission to tease them. As adults we just do it. As a result children become more and more closed and uncommunicative in order to protect their feelings. If we want our children to feel free to come to us with their problems, we must stop teasing them. If other adults tease our children, we can often stop them by merely stating, "We don't tease our children."

Children often complain to parents about being teased at school. It is important to ask children if they have ever teased, and if so, what were they feeling? Usually the answer is "I was feeling bad." Then it is simple for a child to understand what the teaser is feeling. This gives them the opportunity to handle the teaser by making simple statements like "Are you having a bad day"? It is important to realize that humans do not hurt others unless they themselves are hurting.

TICKLING—PHYSICAL RIDICULE

> The best tickler impersonates an aggressor, but is simultaneously known not to be one!
>
> —*Arthur Koestler*

Like teasing, tickling is an unclear and manipulative form of communication because it depends on the recipient being uncomfortable. When I ask the people in my groups how many have been sat on and tickled, I am astonished by the numbers who raise their hands with moans and groans.

Of all the forms of ridicule, tickling is the most obvious enactment of control and manipulation. If you watch someone who is being tickled, all of their physical responses have to do with defending themselves from an attack. Though the attack in this instance is not intended to be violent, it nonetheless invades our personal space and stimulates the lighter levels of fear and anger.

It is impossible to tickle ourselves. Therefore, tickling has to do with an interaction between two or more persons, and it creates tension which is then expected to be released in laughter. Between consenting peers, tickling is not hurtful and can be very enjoyable, but most frequently tickling occurs without permission between people of different physical sizes and/or strengths. When children are sat upon and tickled, they sometimes become so distressed that they burst into tears, at which point the tickler usually withdraws.

OOTSY, GOOTSY, GOO

> Even tickling can be violent. Sadly, our culture doesn't teach people to be sensitive to the feelings of others. Tickling can be quite painful.
>
> —*Dr. Thomas Radecki*

I was standing with a woman friend and her baby in a stroller. A mutual acquaintance of ours came over and, upon seeing the baby, reached down with his hand, grabbed the baby's stomach, and went, "Ootsy, gootsy, goo!" The child immediately began screaming and the mother, obviously embarrassed, apologized, saying that the baby was tired and cross. She implied that otherwise the child would have laughed, when in fact the child was reacting to a sudden and terrifying invasion.

When my own children were babies, I used to tickle them in order to get them to laugh. I believed that their laughter meant they were happy, and if my babies were happy, then I was a good mother.

I think adults who have the urge to tickle children need to examine where that urge comes from. Perhaps it is the need to exert power, the need to have a happy child, the need to have the child laugh so that we can then laugh, or simply to make contact. Some of us are embarrassed about outward shows of affection and use tickling in order to make physical contact with our children. If this is the case, very often we can substitute a hug or simply hold the child as a much more tender, direct, and loving form of physical communication.

TRICKS FOR TENDER TICKLING

Many people who hear my tickling theory become very upset, thinking that they will no longer have a means to laugh with their children during physical play. This is not my intent. I am not suggesting we eliminate tickling completely; however, as adults, I believe we must be aware of the messages we give our children and the power we exert over them. We often treat our children the way we were treated. Remembering how we ourselves felt when tickled might be a good starting point for revising how we interact with our own children during tickling.

People often ask me what to do when their children beg to play the tickling game. There are several options.

You can pretend to tickle your child, and the child will laugh just as hard as if really being tickled.

You can put the child in charge of the tickling by making

your hands available but not aggressive, so the child can come to your hands and be tickled as much as he or she needs and yet constantly be in control.

You can substitute other kinds of physical contact—such as hugging, letting the child sit in your lap, or holding the child's hand—to help your child get emotionally healthy physical contact with you, in other ways besides tickling.

You can find other ways to share laughter with your children, such as pillow fights, hiding games, etc. (See Part II, #20, Have a Pillow Fight.)

LAUGHTER DOESN'T HAVE TO HURT

> I don't know what humor is. Anything that's funny—tragedy or anything, it don't make no difference so (long as) you happen to hit it just right. But there's one thing I'm proud of—I ain't got it in for anybody. I don't like to make jokes that hurt anybody.
>
> —*Will Rogers*

One of the most popular TV programs of the seventies was "All in the Family" featuring the character Archie Bunker who was the ultimate racist, sexist, "et cetarist." Somehow this show was revered as a valuable example of dealing with these issues through laughter. Actually, we were seduced into ridicule in a very insidious way. By ridiculing the ridiculer (Archie) and by laughing at his put-downs, we joined him in becoming part of the problem instead of part of the solution.

In a recent interview, Lily Tomlin reflected on a similar phenomenon with the play, The Comedians. She said that this play "allows people to laugh at racist and sexist jokes without any real awareness that they are doing so."

I saw a wonderful interview on Phil Donahue's show with Bill Cosby and a Harvard psychiatrist named Alvin Poussant. Poussant had been hired by the "Cosby Show" to screen all scripts for ridicule. When Phil Donahue asked Cosby why he had a permanent staff member to do this, Cosby replied that as a comedian he tended to go for the laughs without thinking clearly about the hurt the laughter might bring. It is not by chance that the "Cosby Show" was the number one television show for so many years. After viewing it, we have a warm cozy feeling about family life. This is in direct contrast to the majority of sitcoms on television which rely on put-downs and laughter at another person's expense.

If ridicule worked, we would all be in great shape. As it is, jokes, teasing, and tickling often add fuel to the fires of fear, anger, and resentment. It is unfortunate that the majority of the humor in our culture falls into the category of ridicule. This keeps us disconnected, insecure and anxious about potential hurt from one another. As we begin to rekindle the laughter we engaged in as infants and small children we re-enter the realm of healing and connecting laughter. (For ways we can bring healing laughter into our lives, see Part II).

CHAPTER 4

Grown-ups Don't Holler OW! Laughter & Physical Pain

I never saw anything funny that wasn't terrible.

—*W.C. Fields*

Dorothy, an athletic woman in her thirties, volunteered to work on her physical pain at one of my workshops. She explained that she had had a pain in her shoulder ever since she fell while skiing five weeks before. I asked how she felt about having an injured shoulder. "Like a cripple," she answered.

"Are you angry at your shoulder for hurting so long?" I asked. "Have you been sending negative messages to your shoulder? Telling it what a bad shoulder it is?" She laughed, and nodded in agreement.

I explained that her negative thoughts about her shoulder caused more physical tension, which resulted in more pain and slower healing. I suggested that Dorothy touch her shoulder and send some tender messages to it, such as, "You're a good shoulder, you're a real nice shoulder." Of course, when she did this, she couldn't help laughing.

I wanted Dorothy to get in touch with her pain, to bring it

out and play with it. So I suggested that she gently twist her shoulder until it hurt. She gave me a strange look, so I cautioned her not to reinjure it, but just to move it around until she could feel the pain. She rotated the shoulder gingerly until she winced.

"Good! Now do it again—feel the pain. And when that happens, I want you to yell out at the top of your lungs, OW!"

Dorothy and the entire audience laughed at this instruction. Then she rotated her shoulder and let out a tentative "OW!"

"Louder still."

"OWW!"

"Again."

"OWWW!"

Each time Dorothy shouted out in pain, she followed it with an embarrassed laugh. In fact, the louder she OWed, the harder she laughed, until the whole room was roaring. She was laughing—we all were laughing—with the contagion of grown-ups who don't holler "OW!" (especially in public places). That was the point of the exercise: to get her to laugh and release the tension that was contributing to the pain in her shoulder.

"In order to release pain," I told her, "you first have to let yourself experience it. That's what the pain is for: it tells you where you need to focus your attention."

"It's amazing," Dorothy said, "because I can't feel the pain when I'm laughing!" Each time Dorothy did the exercise, she had to turn her shoulder a little more in order to experience the pain. After repeating this exercise for five minutes, Dorothy reported that her shoulder felt quite a bit better. Dorothy's experience is an example of how adults can confront and work on physical pain through laughter.

THE RELATIONSHIP BETWEEN PAIN, TENSION, AND LAUGHTER

> Even in laughter the heart is sorrowful.
>
> —*Proverbs 14: 13*

Acknowledging our pain is the opposite of what we're taught. We learn to avoid pain by denial, diversion, or drugs. Most of our pain comes not so much from the injury itself, but from the tension we build up trying to avoid feeling it, and from the negative messages we inflict on ourselves because we're hurting . . . this becomes suffering. Additional tension is created from the fear of what the pain might mean (i.e. cancer, heart attack, death, etc.). When we laugh we release the tension we need to release. The pain, as in Dorothy's case, is a focal point that directs the laughter to move to where the tension needs releasing. Once this occurs, our bodies' natural healing mechanisms have a direct shot at the traumatized area.

No one knows the relationship between laughter and pain better than professional comedians. They understand that just as our muscles tense up around areas of physical trauma, our muscles also tense up around areas of emotional distress. These people make their living simply by reading the newspapers and holding up the headlines to us in a playful way that triggers our collective laughter.

Aside from paid comedians, our society treats pain as an enemy. If we hurt, we are advised to eliminate the pain with an aspirin. Or we're encouraged by a famous, retired athlete to wash away tension with a few beers. And if the pain persists, we're told to get a prescription for a heavy-duty painkiller. When we take this advice (although sometimes it is necessary), we stifle our natural capacities for self-healing.

People who are on tranquilizers have difficulty laughing and crying. We have to be at least a little bit uncomfortable in order to laugh. Adults have been conditioned to deny discomfort and pain. Children, when they are hurt, nearly always cry. Many adults are aware of their need to cry as well, but because of cultural taboos, laughter (probably from embarrassment of admitting pain) is more readily available.

PAIN IS POSITIVE

> They laugh often with tears in their eyes.
>
> —*W.C. Fields*

Pain is our friend. It is our warning system and an ally against disease, destruction, and death. Pain notifies us that something is amiss. It's a red flag that calls out: "Yoo hoo! Pay attention—over here!"

Hansen's disease (leprosy) blocks the sensation of pain. Victims fall prey to accidents and infection because they can't feel physical pain and are therefore unaware of injuries to their bodies. This is an extreme example of the necessity of pain for survival.

The human organism was ingeniously designed to receive sensory information from its various parts and to process it in a way that will sustain our good health. Drugging, denying, and diverting pain allow it to accumulate in our bodies as stress chemistry.

I try to help people confront their accumulated pain in a playful way, so that the tension surrounding the pain is released as laughter. I never play with someone else's pain; that would be control, manipulation, or ridicule. Rather, I support and educate people in identifying and playing with their own pain, and, with permission, I give them suggestions that help them do this.

THE "OW" AND LAUGHTER TECHNIQUE

> There isn't much fun in medicine but there's a great deal of medicine in fun.
>
> —*Journal of the American Medical Association*

Many people think that the "OW" and laughter technique works only with relatively minor pain. This technique can be used even in a hospital setting.

Bob, a man in his fifties, had been a client of mine for some time. He discovered that he had a tumor on his knee that required surgery. Bob was aware of the power of laughter in the healing process. In consulting with me, he agreed that a local anesthetic would be to his advantage. In addition, I pointed out that a private room would allow him to work with unorthodox methods more freely, and because of his financial situation, he was able to arrange this.

I appeared in his room directly after the surgery. Because Bob had insisted on a local anesthetic, he was awake, alert, and ready to work. Bob had an incision on the inside of his leg around the knee area that measured between 10 and 12 inches in length. His knee was wrapped in such a manner that he was able to remove a portion of the outer bandage. I had him press very lightly around the incision area and say, "OW!" We had a pillow ready so that in case a big "OW!" came out, he could stifle the sound and not alarm the hospital staff.

As he pressed around the incision and said "OW!" he laughed. The more he pressed and the more he said "OW!" the harder he laughed. In between the laughter, he related the events of the surgery. By processing the emotions that occurred during surgery, he prevented that tension from storing around the traumatized area, and allowed his body's healing mechanisms to function faster and more freely.

After about half an hour, it was taking more and more pressure for him to feel any pain. At this point, the surgeon came in to see how Bob was doing. He came toward the bed and said, "Bob, how are you feeling?" Bob kicked out his leg. The surgeon was so shocked that he almost fell over backward. I learned later that Bob was on his feet walking around the hall within several hours. He reported that the surgeon was astounded by the rate of his recovery.

Because the "OW" and laughter technique falls outside of the traditional training physicians have received, information about this procedure is difficult for them to hear. As a result, I am cautious about sharing these techniques with my clients' doctors. If you want to try this technique in a hospital setting, it is very important either to have complete privacy or, if that is not possible, to share enough information with roommates so that they can cooperate and learn from the process. The nurses very often are supportive. Because they perform the hands-on care of patients, they are more receptive to the need for emotional release.

"I WAS IN STITCHES": HEALING THE HURT THROUGH LAUGHTER

> Mirth is God's medicine.
>
> —*Henry Ward Beecher*

A colleague called me one day and asked if I would go and see his mother. "She's in her eighties," he said, "and she lives by herself. Lately she's been crying a lot. She'll burst into tears while she's walking down the street, at the breakfast table, or in the supermarket, and it bothers her. She could probably use some counseling, but I'm not the one to do it." I made an appointment to see Rosie at her apartment.

The minute she opened the door I could tell I was going to enjoy her. Rosie had a wonderful twinkle in her eye. She was a tiny woman, with wispy white hair and dark blue eyes. She looked physically fragile, yet her attitude was tough as nails.

As we sat down, I asked Rosie to tell me about herself. She told me she was born in Leningrad and had emigrated to the United States when she was eleven. She grew up on the lower east side of New York, worked as a seamstress in the garment district, and was involved in the labor movement. I was intrigued by her story; her life seemed like a novel encompassing much of the twentieth century.

Rosie was pleased to have an eager listener, and for the next few sessions she went back over her eighty-three years, looking at the pieces and fitting them together. She laughed when she remembered the good times and cried when she remembered the bad—and sometimes it was the other way around.

"I never allowed myself to cry," she told me, weeping now. "I always had to be strong." The backlog of feeling was so great that she couldn't contain it any longer. I told her that it was all right for her to cry; it was natural, understandable, and apparently unavoidable. So we cried, and we laughed. Laughter was easy for her, because Rosie had always been a laugher.

We worked together once a week for a month, and Rosie's crying gradually began to subside. There was no longer a need to continue seeing her.

Three months later her son called to tell me she was in the hospital. She had fallen and broken her hip, been operated on, and then had undergone a second operation to remove some lesions in her intestines. Her son said she wanted to see me.

I went to the hospital and found her lying in bed asleep. She was plugged into tubes, wires, and machines and was herself just a slight bump under the bedsheets.

I put my hand on her forehead, and she opened her eyes. When she saw me, she started to cry. She cried for about two minutes, silently, and then she tried to say something. I couldn't understand what she was saying because she didn't have her teeth in.

As I bent down closer, barely making out the words, I realized it was a dirty joke. Rosie dissolved into laughter when she was finished, and I had no choice but to laugh along with her.

She laughed so hard that, as she explained a few minutes later, "I don't know where to hold myself!" She had a great many stitches and she was sore all over.

By the time I left the room, Rosie had laughed over one thing or another for fifteen or twenty minutes. She knew, intuitively, that she needed to do this. When I went to see her again two days later she was ready to laugh some more. Surprisingly, she was in a wheelchair already, exploring the hallways with her IV bottles dangling over her head. We went down to the sunroom where we could be alone, and she told me more stories from her childhood, and she laughed and laughed and laughed.

She was released from the hospital a week later. Her son told me her doctors were astonished at her quick recovery, considering her advanced age and condition.

HOSPITALS NEED TOYS, TOO

> The art of medicine consists of amusing the patient while nature cures the disease.
>
> —*Voltaire*

Toys are very useful in a hospital because of the serious nature of the events that happen there. Some years ago, my mother had a stroke. On my way to the hospital, I stopped at a toy store and bought a cute, battery-operated dog. This little dog, when it was turned on, would walk along, bark, sit down, bark, stand up and walk along again. It repeated this cycle over and over until the batteries wore out. The toy store had these little dogs on long leashes, barking, sitting, walking, and generally delighting all who saw them.

I knew my mother would love the little dog because we had

always had dogs in our family. During the depression, she raised puppies as a way of bringing additional income into the family. When I got to the hospital and put the batteries in the dog, turned it on, and put it on the floor for her to see, it malfunctioned. Instead of going through its expected cycle, it barked, sat down, and scooted. When my mother saw this happen, she began to laugh and we all laughed with her. Those of us who have been around puppies know that when they scoot, it means they have worms. So this malfunction struck an extra chord of hilarity. The nurse ran in to see what the commotion was about, saw the little dog and began laughing. She took the dog out into the hall and let it loose. This in turn brought patients out of their rooms to join in the fun.

Bill was a student in my laughter class who came to me with a specific problem. He had had a hernia operation ten years before that had been very traumatic and painful—and he had recently discovered that he needed another one. Bill was frightened and wanted to know how he might handle the operation differently this time.

I suggested to Bill that he buy some small wind-up toys. He bought three or four little wind-up and pop-over animals that would easily slip under his hospital gown. He was actually able to sneak them into the operating room. Before the anesthetic was administered, he brought them out, wound them up, and had them running around on the gurney doing their respective tricks. The surgeon became entranced with them, started laughing, wound them up, and had them running around, prompting the nurses and the anesthesiologist to join in. There was a great deal of laughter as a result.

Bill remembers going under the anesthetic peacefully and with a smile on his face. He succeeded in transforming what had been a very painful past experience, into a relatively pleasant one. Needless to say, I am sure the physicians were delighted to have that extra laugh, and if there is anything we want during surgery, it is relaxed surgeons.

Hospitals are traumatic places for everyone.

TROY'S NINE MUMMIES

Fling but a stone, the giant dies. Laugh and be well.
—*Matthew Green*

Troy was six when he was brought to me by his parents because he was having nightmares that woke him up and left him terrified. His mother said that the dreams were about mummies. She believed they might have something to do with two operations that Troy had had when he was younger.

At our first session Troy and I talked briefly about these nightmares, and then I had him draw a picture of them. He drew nine mummies standing around a table in a room. It seemed his mother was right, because it looked like an operating room. There were also curtains in the background, which could explain why Troy was terrified by the shadows he saw in the draperies at home.

"When I was your age," I told him, "I used to go to the movies with my friends on Saturday afternoons, and the movies I remember best were the ones about a mummy. One was called *The Mummy Arises From the Dead,* one was called *The Mummy Speaks,* and another one was *The Mummy's Revenge.* They were very scary movies! When we'd walk home from the movies, my friends and I would act like the mummy . . . all wrapped up, one arm reaching out, one leg dragging behind—like this."

I gave him a demonstration, trying to look as mummified as I could.

He sat with his knees pulled up under his chin, small, blond, and defenseless, and watching me with his big eyes.

"What would you like to do to those mummies in your picture?" I asked him.

He thought about it. "Get rid of 'em," he murmured.

"How?"

He shrugged his shoulders.

"Okay," I said, "let's try it. I'll be the mummy again, and I'm going to come after you. Just like they do in your dreams!"

"That's when I always wake up," he said.

"When they're just about to get you?"

"Yeah."

"Well, let's pretend. Let's see if you can get rid of the mummy." I stood up and began to move toward him, very slowly, one arm reaching out and one leg dragging behind. At first Troy cringed, scrunching even lower in his chair. He hid behind his knees. When I was standing over him, he cried "Go away!" and closed his eyes.

"Aaaarghhh," I growled.

Suddenly he sat up, and he pointed his finger at me. "Bang! Bang!" he shouted. "You're dead!"

I gasped and clutched at my heart. Slowly, I crumpled to the floor. Troy burst out laughing. He loved this game, so we played it again.

I returned to my chair, then rose from it as the mummy, and advanced toward him. This time Troy knew what to do. He let me get just close enough to frighten him, and then he whipped out his gun. "Bam! Bam! Bam!"

We did this three times during the first session, and each time I died dramatically. At the end of the first session, I asked Troy to draw another picture of the nightmare. There were only six mummies left.

When he came to see me the next week, he was eager to play the game again. He created new ways of killing me. He drove an imaginary knife into my heart, he pretended to hurl me out of the window, he tackled me and sat on my head. Each time he laughed wildly and fiendishly, with bravery. We killed off three additional mummies during the second session. His drawing of the dream showed only three left.

My work with Troy confirmed his mother's belief that his nightmares were related to his surgeries. I believe they stemmed from his sense of helplessness. His experience as a patient, particularly as a young patient, left him feeling powerless and frightened. Our exercises showed he was angry about being made powerless. By allowing him to "kill" me I showed Troy that he could act on his own behalf. I reminded him he did have power. The laughter served its crucial purpose of releasing his bottled-up fear and anger.

During the third session Troy killed off the last of his mummies. After that, his nightmares disappeared, and so did his fear of shadows in the curtains.

TAKING CHARGE AS A PATIENT

> What I call a good patient is one who, having found a good physician, sticks to him till he dies.
>
> —*Oliver Wendell Holmes*

We go to hospitals for specific needs to be met, but we also need to take charge of our own patient care and insist that we get the kind of care that makes sense for us. In the United States, most hospitals, both architecturally and in their actual procedures, are designed for the convenience of those who work there rather than the patients. As a result we need, as patients, to be alert and thoughtful when we enter this environment.

In the early seventies, I needed to have a D&C. The procedure was such that it could be done on an outpatient basis. I arranged with my gynecologist to have a local anesthetic so I could be alert and aware during the process. He agreed and set the date.

At dawn, as my friend was driving me to the hospital, I began to cry. I cried (for whatever reason) for the twenty-minute ride. After I got to the hospital, undressed, and climbed into bed, the nurse came in and took my blood pressure. She looked at me with great alarm and took my blood pressure again. She quickly left the room and returned with the physician, who then took my blood pressure, looked at me quisically, and told me that if I were any more relaxed I would be dead. I had had no drugs at this point, but the crying had so relaxed me and rebalanced the chemistry from my stress that my blood pressure was unusual for someone anticipating surgery.

The physician told me that I was to have a general anesthetic. I said no. He said that a general anesthetic was hospital policy. I matter-of-factly told him that if I couldn't have a local, I would go home. He excused himself a minute, left the room, came back and said, "Okay." I also refused any medication to calm me, since I was about as calm as anybody could get.

I was put on the gurney and rolled into the elevator and down to the surgical floor. As they rolled me down the hall, I spoke to the green-clothed mummies walking past me. Each time I spoke, they showed obvious surprise. I realized that on the surgery floor, patients are not expected to be alert and aware.

The nurses parked me in the hall and left. As I lay on my back by myself in this place, I felt very vulnerable. My fear began to surface. I felt helpless and scared about the upcoming surgery. I could hear noises down the hall, so I proceeded to propel myself forward by placing one hand over the other, pushing myself along the wall toward the sounds. As my cart rolled into a doorway, I could see that it was an operating room with nurses preparing, as it turned out, for my own surgery. I was able to talk and laugh and chat with them while they were doing their work and I felt a great deal better.

As they put me on the operating table, I asked the anesthesiologist to tell me everything that he was doing. As he put the needle in my back for the spinal and described the procedure, I said, "Oh, I didn't even feel that. My goodness, you do a good job. You're terrific at this." He hemmed and hawed and then said, "Gee, it's really nice being able to talk to you." I realized that the patients he deals with are unconscious or drugged, so he can't have an aware conversation with them, much less receive any positive feedback. I asked him if he would hold my hand during the procedure just to reassure me, and he was delighted. We had wonderful exchanges throughout the half hour I spent in the operating room.

After the surgery was over, I was rolled into the recovery room. There were about seven other patients lying on gurneys, all of whom were unconscious. The nurses were scurrying about. When patients were due to come out of their anesthesia, the nurses would shout and yell to awaken them. I was astounded by the almost angry way this was done, and watched carefully as they did this. I watched them so closely that it made them self-conscious, so they rolled me into a far corner of the room and surrounded my gurney with a curtain. This isolated me so that I was unable to see what was going on, even though I could still hear it. I am convinced that they felt some guilt in the way they were treating patients. As a patient, I wouldn't want to wake up if I were being treated in this manner.

Feelings of isolation and loneliness swept over me as I lay on my back, unable to move my legs, waiting for the anesthetic to wear off. I kept calling the nurses to put me back in my room. They refused, saying that the physician would have to okay it, yet they neglected to contact the physician. I felt very helpless, very powerless, and very young.

At this point, a friend who is notorious for her nerve opened the recovery room door. The nurses scurried over and told her that no visitors were allowed. She said, "But I am her personal counselor!" (She lied.) They were caught so off guard that they said, "Oh, okay," and in she came to my curtained alcove.

As soon as I saw her, we started to laugh. Immediately the nurses caught on and made her leave, but it was too late. I couldn't stop laughing. I laughed and laughed and laughed, all by myself, lying flat on my back, surrounded by what the nurses had hoped to be a separating wall. I was laughing so hard that they immediately wheeled me out of the room and upstairs to my bed, without waiting for the physician's okay. So I truly laughed my way out of the recovery room. As patients, we can take charge of our hospital stays, making them the way we need them to be.

HOME HEALING THROUGH LAUGHTER AND TEARS

> To whom should I go for some Self Help? I'm not always depressed: only when I think or when I feel.
>
> —*Ashleigh Brilliant*

If you miss the opportunity to use laughter in the hospital, it is possible to laugh and cry at home. I received the following letter from a client's husband:

> Dear Annette,
>
> I have never been one to cry or show my emotions about things that have happened to me during my life. I have felt anger, sadness, and joy, of course, but for the most part I have hidden these feelings.
>
> When I was young, I hurt my back and I have had problems all my life with periodic pain and discomfort. In June of this year, it finally let go and I ruptured a disc in my lower back. Never have I felt such pain as I had in my back and leg.

After an operation, I went home to rest and recover. I expected to be out the next day, leaping tall buildings at a single bound. That did not happen. The pain, although less, went on. What with that and the side effects of the pills I was taking, I became worried and depressed. I worried that I would not get better and what would happen to me.

One Saturday morning, three weeks after the operation, I had a lot of pain and I felt quite low. Suddenly I started to cry and never have I cried so much. The memories of things past flooded back and I found myself crying for things that had happened during World War II, and that was fifty years ago.

As I cried I began to relax and to breathe deeply and then to physically feel better. Gradually my crying changed to laughter and soon I was laughing out loud. The more I laughed the more I relaxed, and the pain and stress just seemed to melt away. The laughing again changed to crying but not as deeply as the first time. I had to go to Los Gatos that morning and I laughed and giggled all the way there feeling good all the time.

For a long time I have not been able to sleep well at night. I would very often wake up early in the morning and sometimes lie awake for an hour or more. Since the crying and laughing episode, I have been able to sleep well every night, perhaps there is a connection.

It is hard to believe the power that laughter has in physical healing, especially when it is tied in with such a painful condition as surgery. One thing to remember is that stitches are strongest when fresh so we don't have to worry about splitting our stitches when we laugh. Of course, they also hurt more then, too. But this once again pinpoints our attention, through laughter and crying, to where it needs to be so that the healing takes place rapidly.

CHAPTER 5

The Physical Body of Laughter

> Laughter is the sensation of feeling good all over, and showing it principally in one place.
>
> —*Josh Billings*

A Victorian medical journal describes the physiology of laughter as follows:

> There occur in laughter and more or less in smiling, colonic spasms of the diaphragm in number ordinarily about eighteen perhaps, and contraction of most of the muscles of the face. The upper side of the mouth and its corners are drawn upward. The upper eyelid is elevated, as are also, to some extent, the brows, the skin over the glabella, and the upper lip, while the skin at the outer canthi of the eyes is characteristically puckered. The nostrils are moderately dilated and drawn upward, the tongue slightly extended, and the cheeks distended and drawn somewhat upward; in persons with the pinnal muscles largely developed, the pinnae tend to incline forward. The lower jaw vibrates or is somewhat withdrawn (doubtless to afford all possible air to the distending lungs), and the head, in extreme laughter, is thrown backward; the trunk is straightened even to the beginning of bending backward, until (and this usually happens soon), fatigue-pain in the diaphragm and accessory abdominal muscles causes a marked proper flexion of the trunk for its relief.

> The while arterial vascular system is dilated, with consequent blushing from the effect on the dermal capillaries of the face and neck, and at times of the scalp and hands. From this same cause in the main the eyes often slightly bulge forward and the lachrymal gland becomes active, ordinarily to a degree only to cause a "brightening" of the eyes, but often to such an extent that the tears overflow entirely their proper channels." (Taken from Ray Moody's *Laugh After Laugh, the Healing Power of Humor*.)

Examining the physiology of laughter reminds us how profound a process laughing is. Laughter engages every major system in the body. When I do my presentations on the physiology of laughter, I always bring someone up on the stage to laugh with me for two or three minutes, for no apparent reason. I assign the audience the task of observing what goes on with us physiologically as we are laughing. Not many people realize that two to three minutes of laughter is a very, very long time. Nearly always, the person who has agreed to join me keeps asking, is it time yet, is it time?

THE LOSS OF MUSCLE CONTROL

> The old man laughed loud and joyously, shook up the details of his anatomy from head to foot, and ended by saying that such a laugh was money in a man's pocket, because it cut down the doctor's bills like everything.
>
> *"Tom Sawyer" by Mark Twain*

After the laughter is over, I ask the audience for their observations. Almost without exception, the first thing they notice is that we bent over and moved around a lot. When we laugh, we literally lose muscle control. That is why we fall out of our chairs laughing. That is why we can't hold a pencil in order to write while we are laughing. It is why, as kids, we fall down on the floor laughing and spitting out food from our mouths. And it is why we wet our pants when we laugh.

As I tell these things to the audience, and ask if they have had these experiences, nearly everyone raises their hand. Everyone has stories about the helplessness they have experienced during a bout of laughter. We even use the expression, "I was helpless with laughter."

Scientists are studying pygmies because it has been observed that all pygmies fall down on the ground when they laugh. I believe that all of us, if we were truly free, without controls and restrictions on the way we laugh, would fall down every time we laugh.

A dear friend who was a Plains Cree Indian told me that in his tribe everyone leans on something when they laugh. Apparently the Plains Indians have fewer restrictions than those of us who are white, yet more restrictions than the pygmies. Imagine what life would be like if we all fell down every time we laughed!

In my advanced laughter class, we practiced falling out of our chairs laughing on at least one evening per term. We did this in order to get through the embarrassment of falling on the floor, just in case we might need to someday. Needless to say, when we do this, very often we kick up our heels and show things we are not supposed to show. We are not acting in a culturally approved manner; we are literally not in control of ourselves. Laughter is indeed the loss of control.

Many comedians learned their art of comedy on the streets of a big city, where they observed that, if you keep people laughing, they can't hurt you. When approached by a bully who threatens physical harm, the comedian creates laughter, which in turn prevents the bully from beating up on him, since he has lost muscle control. Unfortunately, some comedians can't turn this skill off, so any time they feel tension they crack a joke or act funny. Those of us with friends who do this know that it is difficult to interact with them.

My favorite story about laughter and the loss of muscle control happened some years ago when I gave my first television interview. I was called by the local CBS station, and the interviewer explained to me that we would have six minutes for the interview, less the two minutes for a commercial, for a total of approximately four minutes. He explained that I would be on live on the noon news and made arrangements for when I would come.

When the day rolled around, I still had no idea what I was going to say in four minutes. By the time the interviewer began to introduce me, the tension I was feeling, to put it mildly, was intense. I began to laugh, which I often do when I am feeling the tension of embarrassment. The camera was on the interviewer, but the audience could hear me laughing. He kept looking over at me, and every time he did, I would laugh harder. He started laughing, and as a result, he began slipping out of his chair, almost to the floor. As he did this I laughed harder, he laughed harder, and the interview was obviously not going the way he had planned.

At one point, he reached over and touched my arm and said, "But seriously, Annette," and of course, I started laughing even harder. I think throughout the whole four minutes I said one word in answer to his questions. All during this interview, he had to revive himself from the prospect of becoming a helpless mass of uncontrolled muscles. While all this was going on the cameramen were also laughing.

In reflecting on this experience, I realized that I had conveyed to the audience all the important information I had wanted to say about laughter by allowing the interviewer to be an example of my topic. The interviewer demonstrated all the aspects of laughter that I would have wanted to sum up, so the experience was a highly instructive one, not only for the audience but for myself as well. What better way to illustrate the connection between laughter and the loss of muscle control?

I thought for sure that my career with CBS was down the tubes, and reassured myself that there were other networks. As the interviewer walked me to my car and thanked me for coming, he eagerly invited me back to do the evening news!

There are some important things that should not be done while laughing, due to the resulting lack of muscle control. A dancer friend remarked that no jokes are allowed during ballet rehearsal when the partners are being lifted, for obvious reasons. A friend of mine has always said that it is very dangerous to move a refrigerator upstairs while you are laughing. A woman in my advanced laughter class reported that she and a sister were trying to move a mattress upstairs. They would get to laughing because they couldn't fit it around the landing. The more they laughed, of course, the less they could hold onto the mattress. They would drop the mattress, it would slide down the stairs, and with great glee, they would jump on the mattress and ride it down. She said it took them forty-five minutes to get the mattress up the stairs.

Laughter itself is a delightful form of whole body relaxation. A yoga teacher told me that he begins his classes by getting his students to laugh. Only when their muscles are relaxed can they do the rather preposterous postures that he requires, and enjoy them at the same time.

Since I started doing laughter work publicly, I have started wearing skirts. I encourage women who want to take up laughter as a daily habit to reconsider their wardrobe. I always laugh a lot and usually wet my pants two or three times during any presentation. Little panty liners are very helpful to stem the embarrassment that I might otherwise experience in this situation. I don't have a solution for men who wish to take up laughter, but being a creative lot, I know that they will find one.

CONVULSING THE DIAPHRAGM

> Laugh (n). A smile that burst.
>
> —*John Donovan*

It seldom fails that when myself and a volunteer from the audience are demonstrating laughter on stage, one of us will put a hand over our midsection. When we laugh, our diaphragms convulse. We have some common sayings that reflect this: "I laughed so hard my sides split," or "I had a laughing fit," or "I was convulsed with laughter." All of these refer to the convulsive action of the diaphragm.

The diaphragm is the muscle that separates our abdominal cavity from our chest cavity, and it is the only muscle in our body that is attached to other muscles. When we laugh, our diaphragm convulsively pulls on our side muscles. Because the diaphragm keeps us breathing, it has been called the muscle of inspiration, and it is certainly the inspiration that keeps us laughing. Laughter gives our diaphragm much-needed exercise that contributes to our inner well-being.

Why is it important to exercise our diaphragm? The main reason is that it creates a massive, massaging action for our innards. No amount of running around the park massages our insides the way laughter does. As our diaphragm automatically convulses, it in turn shakes up our stomach and other vital organs. We get an internal massage, which leaves our organs invigorated, juicy, plumped-up, and alert. We want plump, juicy, alert organs. There are other processes that convulse the diaphragm: hiccuping, coughing, sobbing, and vomiting. Since it is so important to convulse our diaphragm, given the choices, laughter looks pretty good.

DILATING THE CARDIOVASCULAR SYSTEM

> The best doctors in the world are Dr. Diet,
> Dr. Quiet, and Dr. Merryman.
>
> —*Jonathan Swift*

A guaranteed observation from the audience after our on-stage laughter is that our faces turn red. Some people turn red only in blotches, and I've observed that dark-skinned people deepen. When we laugh, our entire cardiovascular system dilates. When people dilate unevenly, they get blotchy.

Initially, when we laugh, our heart rate and blood pressure soar. When we stop laughing they drop below our normal rate. When we don't laugh for a while, we settle back into our normal heart rate and blood pressure. The more you laugh, the greater your ability to lower your heart rate and blood pressure. Adults laugh on the average of fifteen times a day. If you can laugh like a four year old (500 times per day!), you will have the heart rate and blood pressure of a four year old.

Because of the cardiovascular effect of laughter, I have decreased my already-low blood pressure. In fact, my blood pressure is so low that nurses and physicians tend to become alarmed and think that I am about to die. Whenever my blood pressure must be taken, I try to laugh as they are pumping up the armband. By laughing during this procedure, I temporarily elevate my blood pressure and relieve myself of having to reassure and take care of my caregivers.

When we laugh, the circulatory system is exercised by constricting and dilating. As a result, it becomes more flexible. Chronic high blood pressure is partly a matter of the circulatory system being constricted on a fairly permanent basis. Our blood pressure needs to be high on certain occasions: when we are preparing for fight or flight, or when we need to exert ourselves physically. After these situations pass, a healthy cardiovascular system will return our blood pressure to a lower, naturally relaxed state.

It is the exercise and workout of laughter that help keep our cardiovascular system healthy. Just as the heart constricts and relaxes, we experience states of constricted or relaxed musculature throughout our bodies. Probably the best example of these two extremes is the cat. When a cat is uptight, alert, and on guard, its whole system is vertical—its tail is vertical, every pore in its body sends its hair straight up as it hisses and spits. But if you pick up a sleeping cat, you'll notice that ,as you lift it up, it gets longer and longer. You think, "This is the longest cat I've ever seen." You realize that the cat has a tremendous ability to relax. Cats can spring to great heights because of their ability to move quickly between these two states. As humans, we are not able to do that, but we do need to relax and constrict our muscles as our lives demand it. Laughter can help us keep the energy of life pulsating through us so that we can function at an optimum level.

LAUGHTER AND OXYGEN

> When you do laugh, open your mouth wide enough for the noise to get out without squealing, throw your head back as though you were going to be shaved, hold on to your false hair with both hands and then laugh till your soul gets thoroughly rested.
>
> —*Josh Billings*

Someone in the audience always observes that, as we laugh on stage, we inhale massive amounts of air. As we take in air, we gulp large amounts of oxygen, which in our dilated cardiovascular state sends a richly oxygenated blood supply to our relaxed muscles. This contributes to our sense of well-being. Laughter has been clocked exiting our lungs at speeds up to seventy miles an hour. Needless to say, this gives our respiratory system a massive workout.

There are some people who snort when they laugh. This snorting laughter occurs when air is taken in through the nose instead of the mouth. It is always good to have a snorter around because they keep us laughing about our laughter. Instead of making fun of the snorters, we need to cherish and delight in them for the tremendous service they provide.

LAUGHTER AND TEARS

> Those who do not know how to weep with their whole heart don't know how to laugh either.
>
> —*Golda Meir*

It has been observed that when we laugh, our eyes become brighter. This is due to the activation of the lachrymal (tear) glands. And, of course, if we laugh hard enough and long enough, we will cry. Those of us who have laughed so hard we cried know that, in the middle of it, it's very difficult to tell which we are doing. If we are with someone who is laughing so hard that they are about to cry, we often feel awkward because we don't know whether to laugh along with them or suddenly shift our mood to comfort them while they weep. This produces many awkward moments that can be fairly laughable in themselves.

LAUGHTER AND THE BRAIN

> As soon as you have made a thought, laugh at it.
>
> —*Lao Tsu*

Effects of laughter that cannot be observed by an audience are those that occur in the brain. A recent study took special colored pictures (PET scans) of the two hemispheres of the brain while a patient was being stressed (similar to the infrared photos of the earth taken from satellites). The results showed that the right and left brain hemispheres differed considerably in color and pattern. After the patient laughed, the PET scan was repeated and the two hemispheres were found to be almost identical in appearance.

I have felt for years that laughter is a rebalancing process that occurs when we get either too left- or too right-brained. This PET-scan study backs up my intuition. Countless chemicals are produced in our brains and throughout our bodies when we laugh. What seems obvious, and yet is not proved by medical science, is the production of beta-endorphines. These are natural brain opiates and powerful pain relievers. Norman Cousins, in his book *Anatomy of an Illness as Perceived by a Patient,* reported that after fifteen minutes of belly laughter, he could sleep pain-free, drug-free for two hours. He accomplished this in spite of an excruciatingly painful disease.

In 1978, I broke a rib in a motorcycle accident the day before I was due to teach my very first laughter class. I was nervous about teaching my first class at city college (actually, it was the first laughter class taught anywhere), and I knew that in order to set a proper example, I had to laugh. I also knew that if I told the class about my broken rib, it would focus their attention on my pain rather than on my laughter. So I bound my rib with an ace bandage and went to class with great trepidation.

As I started off laughing, it was extremely painful. But after fifteen minutes, the pain subsided and the analgesic affect of the beta-endorphines I had produced lasted a full two hours. Because a broken rib is painful even when breathing, much less laughing, I find this experience an excellent example of the pain-killing properties of laughter.

As the medical world begins to unravel the chemical mysteries of laughter, it will be interesting to follow its progress. So far, medical science has not distinguished between the different kinds of laughter or the chemistry of each. (See Chapter 7 for more details on types of laughter.)

When we sweat (and we do sweat when we laugh), the chemistry of that sweat depends on the type of laughter involved. We know that tears from grief have a different chemical makeup than tears from onions. Even the deodorant industry recognizes the chemical differences in perspiration, and the industry is built on the sweat of fear. (The sweat produced by fear smells different than the sweat from exertion.) The subtleties of these differences are familiar to those who experience them, but the scientific establishment has yet to give attention to this aspect of body chemistry. Research on laughter is only just beginning. I look forward to even more revealing research, which hopefully will back up all my opinions and theories.

THE THYMUS GLAND AND LAUGHTER

> Wrinkles merely indicate where smiles have been.
>
> —*Mark Twain*

Almost without exception, someone in the audience points out that when we laugh our faces move up and down. This is perhaps the most obvious characteristic of the laughing human, and the most neglected scientifically. Nearly all forms of catharsis employ the same muscles in the face that are exercised when we laugh.

There is evidence that these facial muscles have a direct connection to our thymus gland, the master gland of the immune system. Your thymus gland, located right below the upper part of the breastbone, can be found by putting your chin on your chest. It shrinks under stress. When you use the muscles in your face, through laughter, tears, rage, and yawns, the thymus gland relaxes and expands. In its expansive state it functions at its peak. The thymus produces lymphocytes that contain cancer-killing T-cells. T-cells attack the cancer cells that we produce every day and literally rip them apart.

In their groundbreaking work with psychological intervention on cancer, Carl and Stephanie Simonton encouraged their patients to use the process of visualization. Patients visualize their T-cells destroying the cancer cells. The T-cells have been "seen" as killer whales, knights in shining armor, good soldiers, or any number of positive powerful symbols attacking the cancer cells. Visualization helps the brain make even stronger connections with the area in our bodies that need healing.

A woman came to me recently with cervical cancer. She decided to visualize her cancer cells as icky brown spots and her T-cells as white horses. She had the horses charging from her brain off to her cervix to the theme from the *William Tell Overture.* Every time she did this she laughed, further reducing her tension level. Any time she heard or played the music, her healing visualization was triggered.

Unfortunately, by the time we reach adulthood, most of us have only one or two expressions left on our faces—which severely limits our ability to have a positive effect on the thymus. If we are female, our faces are most likely stuck in a permanent smile. This is probably due to the expectation that women should be sweet and pleasant and make everyone feel good by taking care of their feelings. Very often when you ask a person who wears a permanent smile how they are, they answer with a tale of woe, which they relate while maintaining this ridiculous grimace. When I saw my friend Sue and asked her how she was, she said, "I feel terrible. I just lost my job, my boyfriend ran off with my next door neighbor, and my rent is due tomorrow"—smiling all the while.

Men, however, tend to wear a serious, straight expression—one that shows no affect whatsoever. After all, men are regarded as the responsible ones, the people who make the big decisions in our culture. When I saw my friend Sam and asked him, "How are you today Sam?" he responded glumly, "Terrific. I never felt better. I just won a trip to Hawaii. This is the greatest day of my life. I feel fabulous." He said all of this with a perfectly straight, expressionless face.

If we are going to choose a frozen expression, we are probably better off with the grimace. If our faces are fixed in permanent smiles, at least they have to come down to eat and our facial muscles get a little bit of exercise. Remember how your mother used to say that if you don't get that expression off your face, your face will freeze that way? Well, she was right. And, since women live on the average eight years longer than men, that could be why so many of them are walking around with permanent smiles on their faces.

If you can't get your facial muscles to move up and down, there is an alternative way to stimulate the thymus gland. You can thump it. In New Guinea there is a tribe whose members thump their thymus glands every morning upon awakening. (I don't know the name of the tribe, so I just refer to them as the Thymus Thumping Tribe of New Guinea.)

Thumping the thymus is an interesting phenomenon. If we look at the animal world, we find that apes thump their thymuses when they are aroused, excited, or upset. Tarzan was the most famous thymus-thumping human, and he got it from the apes.

But there are other human examples of thymus thumpers. Catholics thump their thymuses while saying, "Mea culpa, mea culpa." (Mea culpa means my fault, my fault, I have sinned.) If we are going to blame ourselves for our actions by saying, "my fault, my fault," we can stay even by thumping the thymus at the same time. This keeps it stimulated instead of shrinking it with negative, stressful thoughts.

Jews also thump their thymuses on Yom Kipper, the day of atoning for one's sins.

I have people thumping their thymuses all over the world. It is one of those things that can be done secretly by turning up the collar on your shirt or pulling your coat up a bit, and thumping your chest very lightly. No one will notice.

A CASE OF THYMUS THERAPY

Laughter makes your thymus plumper
and your circulation stronger.
Laughter stimulates your pumper;
Helps you live a little longer.
Laughter helps you keep your health
and it might increase your wealth:
So, don't let your organs shrivel—
give a smile, a laugh, a giggle!
It improves the atmosphere
and you'll spread a lot of cheer!

—*Mercedes Nelson, RN, BSBA*

My first experience with thymus therapy was with Jerry, who came to me as a client. He had a tumor on his thymus gland that had been medically diagnosed, and he thought that laughter therapy might have an affect on it. He wanted to try many alternative methods before he opted for surgery. When Jerry laughed, his face did not go up. He told me that ever since he got the tumor on his thymus gland, the muscles on the side of his face opposite from the tumor no longer functioned. His eyelid and his mouth drooped considerably. It was so strange to watch him laugh without his face going up, that I suggested he prop his face up when he laughed. I did this purely for my own benefit. I suggested that he continue his laughter exercises at home, which he did, working with the bathroom mirror every morning as he laughed and propped his face up. Jerry's tumor began to shrink, and I always suspected that I had unknowingly interrupted a cycle of physical deterioration by helping him exercise his facial muscles.

THYMUS IRRADIATION

> We bare our teeth in laughter to ease the
> accumulating burdens we bear.
>
> —*Harry F. Harlow*

One of the horror stories of the medical profession involves the thymus gland. Earlier in this century when infants would die suddenly, particularly from crib death, and autopsies were performed, doctors noticed that the thymus glands of these children were very large compared to the thymus glands of adults. They erroneously believed that the cause of death had something to do with the children's large-sized thymus glands, and they even concocted a name for this disease, status thymicolymphaticus.

In his book, *The Body Doesn't Lie,* Dr. John Diamond tells the tale of this concocted disease and how the truth was discovered. During the Korean War, autopsies performed on soldiers killed suddenly on the battlefield revealed that their thymuses were much larger than the thymuses of soldiers who had died after an extended stay in the hospital.

After some exhaustive tests, doctors realized that the thymus gland shrinks during a prolonged illness or period of stress. The prevailing myth had been that most adult thymuses are small because they are no longer needed.

Unfortunately, between the 1920s and '50s, before the thymus was properly understood, doctors got in the habit of irradiating the thymuses of infants to make them smaller. Often these radiation treatments would be given to infants as young as five or six weeks. When I work with large groups, I sometimes ask for a show of hands of people who have had their thymuses irradiated. It is always astounding to see the number of people who have gone through this procedure. Needless to say, it sets them up for cancer of the thyroid because of the proximity of the two glands. All kinds of stress-related illnesses, including cancer, can result in later life because the thymus gland is unable to direct the production of lymphocytes to help curb cancer and other diseases.

Children's thymuses are larger than the thymuses of adults probably because they have not repressed their emotions. They fully use the facial muscles that keep their thymuses expanded and functioning to their fullest. The older we get, the less we use our facial muscles, and the more stress we absorb without releasing and resolving, the smaller our thymuses become.

It is important to note that, when people are alarmed or suddenly startled, they will often put their hand over the thymus part of their chest and say, "Oh!" or "Oh my goodness!" or "Oh my God!" This seems a natural reaction to the sudden shrinking of the thymus gland. Very often when people laugh, they put their hand over their thymus, possibly because they sense the relaxation and expansion happening. When people say "My heart is breaking," they will put both hands over their thymus, when actually their heart is located to the left and much lower. With the truth about the thymus gland revealed, it would behoove us to change the titles of some of our more poignant love songs: "I Left My Thymus in San Francisco," "Thymus-Break Hotel," "Achy Breaky Thymus," and "Peg of My Thymus." Of course, I would have to change my name to Annette Goodthymus.

THYMUS TIPS

> Strange when you come to think of it, that of all countless folk who have lived on this planet, not one is known in history or in legend as having died of laughter.
>
> —*Sir Max Beerbohm*

If you ever want to send your dog or cat into pet nirvana, just tap their thymus gland very lightly. Cats will lean back their heads and their tongues will come out very slightly and their eyeballs will roll up into their heads. Dogs will do a similar kind of thing and their legs will bounce up and down as if you are tickling them. I haven't tried tapping the thymus gland of any other animals, but, depending upon the species, I would do so with extreme caution.

In Southern California, many people wear crystals over their thymus glands in the belief that the crystals will impart some of its magnetic healing power. I recommend that you wear something around your neck while you jog. Most joggers' faces do not jog with them; they maintain serious expressions. But if you wear a pendant or other object at the height of your thymus gland, as you jog the pendant will bounce up and down and stimulate your thymus. If you can move your facial muscles up and down at the same time, you will find that you increase your running time and enjoy it a great deal more. Be aware that a smiling jogger surprises and alarms passersby.

LAUGHTER AND CHEMICAL SUBSTANCES

> Never go to a doctor whose office plants have died.
>
> —*Erma Bombeck*

You might be taking medication that, without your knowing it, is subduing or inhibiting your laughter response. *(Don't terminate your medication without medical supervision!)* Some female hormones, for instance, have this effect, as do certain medications for heart trouble and high blood pressure. The most obvious ones are antidepressants, tranquilizers, sleeping pills, and to some extent, aspirin. Less obvious are those social drugs such as alcohol, cocaine, and marijuana, which stimulate a laughter reflex and condition us to believe that in order to laugh and have a good time, we need drugs.

Those of us who have attended a party and not had anything to drink have witnessed the kind of laughter that alcohol induces. The laughter itself is not contagious for anyone who is not also under the influence. We get the notion that in order to be happy, which means laughing, we must have alcohol to prime the pump. Television commercials show people laughing while holding beer cans or glasses; they won't show people vomiting, driving their cars into trees, or beating up on their kids or each other.

Laughter that is drug-induced is the body's attempt to rebalance the chemistry and tension produced by the effect of the drug. Therefore, it is not cathartic in itself and does not move people in their lives. If we wish to laugh in a way that is truly healing, it must be drug-free.

In order to trigger the release of tension, stress, and pain, we must be able to experience it and feel it. Prescription drugs that alter our moods, as well as the social drugs that we take, have a similar effect: they prevent us from staying in touch with our discomfort and pain. We must allow ourselves to feel some degree of discomfort, which results in tension. The tension can then be released as laughter, and the laughter can have a positive healing effect on the source or cause of the original discomfort. We need to acknowledge and play with our pain in order to laugh.

> Doctors talk a lot about serum cholesterol levels and other measurements. But I think 'serum fun levels' are also important indicators of well-being. We need to raise our serum fun levels if we are to restore and rebalance ourselves. So when you're sick, go home and have fun. Get some positive energy. That's my prescription.
>
> —*David E. Bresler, Ph.D.*

CHAPTER 6

Laughter as Catharsis

> Laughing is just as natural to come to the surface as a rat is to come out of his hole when he wants to. You can't keep it back by swallowing any more than you can the hiccups.
>
> —*Josh Billings*

Mary showed up at one of my laughter workshops, and afterward made an appointment for a private session. Conservatively dressed and formal in manner, she impressed me as a serious person. She confessed to me at the beginning of our session, "I am unable to laugh."

Mary explained that she suffered from colitis. She reported that she and her husband had been trying to have a child for some time, and from all indications there was nothing physical to keep them from conceiving. Mary had been working with a psychiatrist to see if her intestinal pain might have psychosomatic origins. They had uncovered a traumatic childhood incident that seemed to be related. "But nothing has changed," she said. "I've still got colitis and I'm still not pregnant. I'm all tied up inside, like one big knot."

I asked her to tell me about the childhood trauma. Over the period of two sessions, a grisly story came out in bits and pieces.

"I was three years old, as near as I can remember. I was all dressed up in my very best dress. It was pink and frilly and lacy. I had little white anklets with lace around them and my shiny black patent leather shoes on." I could just imagine her with her big blue eyes and blond curls looking like a little angel.

"I was playing with the children next door. I think their parents must have been baby-sitting me. At some point, I left their house and wandered home." She related this to me matter-of-factly, with no emotion.

"When I came home, my mother wasn't there, but there was a man, painting the bathroom. I can't remember just how it happened, or exactly what led up to it. But this painter tried to . . . you know . . . do this thing with me."

"What thing?" I asked.

"Oral sex," she replied. "He wanted me to perform oral sex on him. But when he started to . . ." She paused. She looked puzzled, but then it came to her— "Now I remember! That's how it ended! That's why he didn't go through with it!"

Mary wrinkled up her face in repugnance, as if this had been the greatest shame of all. "I . . . I defecated," she said, "right there on the bathroom floor!"

"Of course you did!" I said. "You were scared!"

"The man got scared, too. So he tried to clean me up. Then he left."

Mary was noticeably relieved to have finally remembered this part of her story. At the next session, she remembered more. "When my mother got home, I tried to tell her what happened, although I didn't have the words to describe it. Now I remember what my mother did! She laughed! Then she said, 'That didn't happen! That couldn't happen to you, Mary. You have a guardian angel! He'd never let a thing like that happen to my little girl!'"

Mary shook her head slowly and looked at me. "Isn't that incredible?" she said. "Not to have believed me, and on top of it to have laughed!" And then she laughed angrily.

I repeated the words for her: "That couldn't have happened to you, because you have a guardian angel!" And she laughed again, even harder.

From a distance of thirty years, Mary could finally see the inappropriateness of her mother's response. At the time, of course, she had been terrified. She was growing up in a strictly religious household and had to assume that she, and she alone, did not have a guardian angel, since she knew she hadn't made up the story.

Mary grew up not wanting or being able to laugh, because laughter had been used by her mother to ridicule and deny her experience. The pain of the terror settled in her bowels. Another consequence was the sexual problem that interfered with her ability to conceive.

It was clear that Mary needed to release the tension in her abdomen that had accumulated around the trauma. We thought laughter could help. We reenacted the exchange between Mary and her mother. I played her mother. Mary couldn't stop laughing at the announcement that it couldn't have happened because she had a guardian angel. After all these years of suppression, the pent-up tension was being released.

MARY'S NEW ANGEL

> Angels fly because they take themselves lightly.
>
> —*G.K. Chesterton*

I asked Mary if she had been able to laugh about the sexual assault itself. She stared at me incredulously, as if to say, you must be crazy. "Absolutely not," she said, and whenever she thought about it she became very depressed.

One of the techniques that therapists use to aid a client to see situations in a different light is called "reframing." In order to help Mary laugh and lift some of her depression, I asked her to reframe this incident, suggesting that, instead of seeing herself as lacking a guardian angel, she imagine telling her mother that she did have an angel, but it was a "shit angel." This "angel" had helped her release her bowels and actually saved her from an even more abusive experience. With the thought that she could tell her mother that she had a "shit angel," Mary's face lit up with rebellious glee and she laughed and laughed and laughed.

Mary and I had several more sessions that consisted of my role-playing her mother. As her mother, I would say that what she told me couldn't possibly have happened, because she had a guardian angel. Her part was to respond, "No, I don't have a guardian angel, I have a shit angel." I, of course, would look shocked and horrified as her very religious mother might have responded. She in turn would laugh with extended peals of deep, rich, angry laughter. Mary was convinced that the tension surrounding the sexual assault was really fear and anger, and that had been obstructing her ability to conceive a child. Her seriousness had been the only way she could control her emotions. Laughter had not been available to her because it had been part of the abuse. We kept repeating this playlet over and over until her laughter finally subsided. We agreed that if she needed to see me again, it would be for a tune-up some time in the future.

Later she wrote to me that her colitis had become very infrequent, and that, lo and behold, she was pregnant. Every Christmas since, I have received a Christmas card with a photograph of Mary and her husband and her little girl.

Mary's experience with laughter is a very good example of what the painful tension of stored anger and fear can do to our lives. In Mary's case, it manifested itself physically, primarily through colitis. It seemed directly connected with her experience at age three. But something else happened to Mary, something nature provided.

Nature controls conception when the environment doesn't seem hospitable to the birth of children. When women are starving or are engaged in excess activity, menstruation ceases. In Mary's case, the tremendous tension created by her pent-up anger and fear certainly would have given her body the message that this might not be a hospitable environment for her to have a child.

WHAT IS CATHARSIS?

> To every thing there is a season, and a time to every purpose under the heaven . . . A time to weep, and a time to laugh; a time to mourn, and a time to dance.
>
> —*Ecclesiastes 3: 4*

Catharsis is the term that I use for Mary's laughter experience. Catharsis is defined in Webster's Dictionary as "the purifying of the emotions or relieving of emotional tension, especially by art, applied originally by Aristotle to the purging of pity or terror by viewing a tragedy . . . [and under psychiatry]—the alleviation of fears, problems and complexes by bringing them to consciousness or giving them expression." The word catharsis was not in common usage until Freud reinstated the term to describe the emotional processes that his first eight female patients went through in order to heal their so-called hysterical symptoms.

People often ask me what approach I use in psychotherapy. If I could put a label on it, I would say I am a very early Freudian. Freud's earliest work was the foundation for the use of catharsis in psychotherapy. Freud thought that when the human being experiences trauma, the nervous system develops and retains an electrical charge. He saw catharsis as the natural way for the body to physically discharge this electrical energy. If the person is not allowed to engage in this process, he or she becomes neurotic. (The words neurotic and neurosis were his invention and come from the word "neuron," which is the cell that transmits electrical impulses along the nervous system.)

As an early Freudian, I find it necessary to give credit for the earliest discovery of our modern view of catharsis to Joseph Breuer, Freud's mentor. Breuer stated: "This [catharsis] was not an innovation of mine, which I imposed on the patient by suggestion. It took me completely by surprise, and not until symptoms had been got rid of in this way in a whole series of instances, did I develop a therapeutic technique out of it."

It is important to note that Breuer did not take credit for instigating cathartic processes. He was adamant about them being natural and curative when allowed to happen without interruption.

Freud worked under Breuer with eight women who had rather extreme "hysterical" symptoms, such as paralyzed arms, inability to drink water, etc. Catharsis relieved almost all of their symptoms. Freud believed that catharsis worked better than hypnosis, the technique he had been using prior to catharsis.

Colleagues often ask me, "Why then did Freud stop using catharsis, and turn to the talk cure?" I explain that when people truly "cathart" from the depths of their being (whether it be through laughter, trembling, crying, or raging), the contagion is so present that if I, the therapist, have not taken care of my own emotions, they too would be triggered by these cathartic processes. My sense of Freud is that he was very controlled. He might have become afraid of his own cathartic needs merely by being in the presence of the process. The other possibility is that about this time he had turned to cocaine with great vigor. Cocaine, a stimulant, draws most people into an action-oriented talkative state, while at the same time it drugs our emotions, effectively stopping catharsis. This would certainly explain his need to use talk therapy rather than cathartic therapy.

While researching my Ph.D. dissertation on laughter, I realized that I was probably the first woman to write about laughter. All the views of laughter were based on theories devised by men. Because men are acculturated to be in control at all times and to deny their emotions, the cathartic theory of laughter is not popular and is found in very few resource books. Freud himself had a very interesting but narrow view of laughter. He believed that laughter results from the repression of sex or hostility. In my experience, this strikes me as a very limited view of laughter, although judging by the majority of jokes told by our comedians, Freud could be considered right on.

CATHARSIS AND CONTROL

> Frequent and loud laughter is the characteristic of folly and ill manners; it is the manner in which the mob express their silly joy at silly things, and they call it being merry. In my mind there is nothing so illiberal and so ill-bred as audible laughter.
>
> —*Earl of Chesterfield*

Because catharsis is profoundly contagious, our culture prevents it, except in very restricted instances. It is okay for us to cry briefly at weddings or funerals, to laugh uproariously at dirty jokes and put-downs in comedy clubs and during our coffee breaks, to laugh and cry into our beer if we are drunk, to exhibit boredom at lectures and concerts, to sweat profusely if we have exerted ourselves physically, to cry if we are women or children (if there is an obvious reason for it), and to fly into uncontrollable dramatic rages that pass for angry outbursts if we are men. People in authority (professionals, employers, and parents), as well as society and its institutions (religion, government, and schools), cannot retain control and allow participants to cathart at the same time.

By the end of 1989, the majority of the world's addicted people lived in the United States. Our need for drugs, including alcohol, prescription and over-the-counter drugs, recreational drugs, caffeine, cigarettes, etc., is unsurpassed in any other population. Drugs are predictors of emotions because when we take a certain drug we know we will feel a certain way. The pressure to be in emotional control at all times and to eliminate all pain sets us up for addiction. What happens is that our lives become uncontrollable as a result of addiction. By attempting to control our emotions through drugs, we lose control of our lives, creating a devastating paradox.

The control of catharsis has some of its roots in survival. Catharsis was controlled in Native American tribes out of necessity, because if a child cried or made any noise while in hiding from a hostile neighbor, the noise might actually result in death. So American Indians stopped their babies from crying by pinching their noses and covering their mouths at the same time. They also taught their dogs not to bark.

We have in our culture a common expression used by women when they see a newborn baby. "Is it a good baby?" they ask, which means literally "Does the baby cry?" If a baby cries, that apparently makes it a "bad baby." Negative judgments on the release of pain (i.e., crying) start at the beginning of life. When a baby cries (and its needs for food and comfort have already been met), it is crying as catharsis. It is very difficult for parents to allow their own children to cathart when they were not allowed to do so as children, and are not allowed to do so now.

LAUGHTER AND EMOTIONAL CONSTIPATION

> Then I commended mirth, because a man hath no better thing under the sun, than to eat, and to drink, and to be merry: for that shall abide with him of his labour the days of his life, which God giveth him under the sun.
>
> —*Ecclesiastes 8: 15*

When I present to a large group, I ask if there is someone in the audience who has worked in a hospital. Nearly always a nurse raises her hand and I ask her how the word cathartic is used in a hospital setting. In the medical world, a cathartic is an enema or laxative. Words like cleansing, purging, and releasing are used to define a cathartic.

Perhaps the best definition of catharsis came to me unexpectedly at a Conference on World Affairs held at the University of Colorado. I was talking with a very elegant East Indian gentleman who was deputy director of a United Nations agency. He laughed throughout our conversation. The combination of his elegant diplomatic appearance, his Oxford-Hindi accent, and his laughter startled me."Mr. Verushi," I said, "you have a wonderful laugh." He ignored my observation and continued to talk and laugh. I repeated myself. He acknowledged me this time and said, "When I was last in India and visited my guru, this is what my guru told me. 'Dreams are the excrement of the mind, feces are the excrement of the body, and laughter is the excrement of the soul.'" I was astounded by the power, earthiness and imagery of this statement, and I responded, saying, "Wow! Now I know what I do. I work with constipation!"

Our culture is emotionally constipated and, as a result, we are dysfunctional. People who work with dysfunctional families know that one of the primary characteristics of these families and its individuals is the denial of emotion. Emotions are repressed, diverted, and oftentimes drugged, which in turn creates rigidity and prevents positive change. Since the word emotion means to move, then anything that stops that movement effectively is constipating. In our language, we refer to an emotional experience as "moving," or we say "I was deeply moved." The films and plays that are most successful are the ones that move us. I refer to the process of catharsis (or the relief of emotional constipation) as having an EM (an emotional movement). A successful EM allows our habits and attitudes to change and become more flexible, adaptable, intelligent, and pro-active.

In spite of extraordinary scientific developments, miraculous machinery, and technological advances, we are becoming more and more aware of our inability to cure certain diseases. We are being forced to look at the person as a whole human being.

Modern medicine has traditionally regarded the human body as a machine separate from mind, spirit, and emotion. Perhaps this is most obvious when we address the area of pain. We often talk about pain as being physiological or emotional, spiritual or intellectual, when actually there is no separation. Pain is pain. In Mary's case, the "emotional" pain of fear had caused an immediate "physiological" response at age three (loss of bowel control); this later developed into the painful "physiological" state of colitis. Her inability to conceive appeared to be connected with the "emotional" pain of anger.

A CALL FOR RESEARCH ON CATHARSIS

> Science (n). An orderly arrangement of what at the moment seem to be facts.
>
> —*Anonymous*

> Technology . . . the knack of so arranging the world that we don't have to experience it.
>
> —*Max Frisch*

The following statement about emotions was made by Candace Pert, Ph.D., former chief of brain biochemistry, clinical neuroscience branch, at the National Institute of Mental Health: "In the beginning of my work, I matter-of-factly presumed that emotions were in the head or the brain. Now I would say, they are really in the body as well. They are expressed in the body and are part of the body. I can no longer make a strong distinction between the brain and the body."

Mary's story is a very good example of what Dr. Pert is referring to. Basically, we are all one piece. Historically, we have had our beings chopped into body/mind/spirit/emotions, with the emotions often being left out totally, so that many groups refer only to body/mind/spirit. Recent developments in the scientific field have led to a new area of investigation called psychoneuroimmunology. Chemicals are produced by the body when we are in pain, whether it be so-called physical or emotional pain. This new field of science, which studies how all our physical and emotional systems are interconnected, will eventually lead to the study of catharsis as a massive, natural, chemical-rebalancing agent.

> It is a very sad thing that nowadays there is so little useless information.
>
> —*Oscar Wilde*

CHAPTER 7

Laugh Your Way Through Three Painful Emotions: Fear, Anger & Boredom

> There are all kinds of humor. Some is derisive, some sympathetic, and some merely whimsical. That is just what makes comedy so much harder to create than serious drama; people laugh in many different ways, and they cry only in one.
>
> —*Groucho Marx*

Many people, including experts in the fields of medicine and psychology, refer to fear, anger, and boredom as negative emotions because they are filled with tension and pain and are unpleasant to experience. But labeling emotions as "positive" and "negative" creates a dilemma. Since emotions are natural and universal, referring to some of them as negative discounts part of our human experience. We actually shut down a necessary part of our healing process—namely, being aware and in touch with our emotions. Unfortunately, in our culture, we are encouraged to deny, divert, and drug our emotions.

THE NATURAL PROCESS OF EMOTION

> If I did not laugh, I think I should die.
>
> —*Abraham Lincoln*

In the natural human process of healing and changing, we "move" our emotions. First we become aware of our painful emotions; then we release the associated tension through the appropriate form of catharsis (such as laughter or tears). We then automatically rethink the situation. Catharsis results in clearer thinking, which in turn enables us to take sensible, more appropriate action. If this natural process is not allowed, we become more and more rigid and reactive, repeating behaviors that are increasingly unsuccessful.

The emotions that are easiest to accept and appreciate are those that are unrelated to pain—such as joy, love, and happiness. These are perhaps misnamed as emotions, since they do not require any movement or action on our part. I believe a more accurate label for them would be "states of being." Our painful emotions create tension in order to move us. Painful emotions are red flags telling us that we need to take some sort of action. We avoid them in much the same way that we avoid physical pain, and yet they are essential to our survival. If we refuse to pay attention, certain painful emotions will go underground and pop up later in different disguises.

CAUTION: UNDERGROUND EMOTIONS

> No man who has once heartily and wholly
> laughed can be altogether irreclaimably bad.
>
> —*Thomas Carlyle*

Fear can become worry, anxiety, or violence. When anger is repressed it may turn into sarcasm, hostility, or hatred. Boredom may turn into hopelessness, helplessness, or apathy. If these emotions are continually repressed, they may become somatic (physical): left to their own devices, they can contribute to, or even cause, physiological problems such as ulcers, asthma, high blood pressure, heart disease, colitis, strokes, or cancer.

It has been my experience and observation that the tension produced by fear, anger, and boredom is released in part by laughter. But, as long as we reject these emotions by labeling them as negative, the laughter that serves as a release of tension will be unavailable to us or will be judged as inappropriate. If we can accept fear, anger, and boredom as being painful instead of negative, we can use laughter to release the tension we feel and become healthier and happier people.

THE SCIENTIFIC METHOD, TEE-HEE

Taken as a whole, the universe is absurd.

—*Walter Savage Landor*

Current research on laughter is very crude, and almost primitive in its concept. It is interesting to note that few researchers make a distinction between laughter and humor. On a recent radio talk show, I was asked about a research study that showed that humor had no effect on the survival rate of middle-aged men with heart disease. Not being familiar with this particular study, I asked the radio interviewer if laughter was involved as well as humor. He was unable to answer. If the subjects were exposed to the researchers' notions of humor, without measuring their laughter or the kind of laughter produced, the study would be ineffective.

People who do research on laughter usually fail to make a distinction between different kinds of laughter. Laughter comes in basically three different forms. There is the so-called nervous laughter resulting from fear; angry laughter (as in Mary's story); and the laughter that rebalances the excruciating pain of boredom. These different laughs produce different responses in the body. They are accompanied by distinct temperatures, varied body chemistries, and different sounds.

THE THREE SOUNDS OF LAUGHTER

He laughed like an irresponsible foetus.

—*T.S. Eliot*

The nervous laughter of fear is high in pitch and staccato in tempo. (It is called a nervous laugh because it makes us nervous to hear it.) When we laugh this way, our bodies are cold and clammy, particularly in our extremities. One place where this kind of laughter commonly occurs is after a fender bender. After information has been exchanged and the police go away, the driver will get back in the car and begin giggling uncontrollably. If there is a passenger in the car, often that person will become uneasy with the driver's seemingly hysterical behavior. We experience discomfort upon hearing nervous laughter because it is poised on the brink of breaking through to the release of deeper fear. The contagion of catharsis is such that, when we hear nervous laughter, it brings up unreleased, stored fears, and keeps us on edge as to what we will be feeling next.

An angry laugh has a distinctive sound. It is often referred to as menacing, evil, or maniacal, and it has a deep and throaty resonance. A woman once told me that her son called this her "mad laugh." The body is warm and sweaty and our faces often turn red.

The third kind of laugh is the laugh that releases the tension or the stress of boredom. This laugh is very musical in its sound and is very attractive and appealing. It's what many children do when they run out into the schoolyard at recess. During this laugh, the body does not seem to sweat or change temperature.

"EEK! A MOUSE!": LAUGHTER AND FEAR

> The biggest laughs are based on the biggest disappointments and the biggest fears.
>
> —*Kurt Vonnegut, Jr.*

Fear is a very important emotion because it prepares us physiologically for fight or flight. When we are afraid, the blood vessels in our extremities constrict in order to drive the blood up into the major muscle groups. Everyone has experienced the physical phenomenon of cold hands and feet. We even have an expression that conveys this very clearly: when someone decides not to get married, we say, "He got cold feet." Laughter is one of the chemical rebalancers of fear. It dilates our cardiovascular system and allows the blood to recirculate to those areas of the body (hands and feet) that are deprived of blood during fear.

FEAR AND TREMBLING

> Laugh out all you trembled out before.
>
> —*William Couper*

In the case of more extreme fear, our bodies tremble in order to recirculate the blood because of the greater and longer constriction of the blood vessels. To be able to run quickly, we don't need blood in our tippy toes, we need it in our calves and thighs. In order to fight and defend ourselves, we do not need blood in our fingertips and hands, we need the blood in our forearms and biceps. Imagine yourself being chased by a grizzly bear. After finding safety, your body trembles in order to recirculate the blood that was driven into your major muscles, mobilizing you to run as fast as you could to save yourself. The body is literally shaking the blood back into the extremities, much like shaking a pillow into a pillowcase in order to fill it.

Most of us have experienced trembling from extreme cold. This is a similar survival response that keeps the blood recirculating so that our fingers and toes (and sometime nose) don't suffer from frostbite. In less severe cases of fear, laughter also recirculates our blood by dilating the cardiovascular system. Remember that nature has provided the constriction of blood vessels in our extremities as a way to defend or remove ourselves when we are in danger. Fear lets us know that we either need to put up a fight or get the hell out of there.

IN SEARCH OF . . . CATHARSIS

> Laugh and the world laughs with you;
> Weep and you weep alone.
> For the sad old earth must borrow its mirth,
> But has trouble enough of its own.
>
> —*Ella Wheeler Wilcox*

Several years ago I was riding a motorcycle when a dog ran onto the freeway directly into my path. I hit him, skidded, and went down. I was not seriously injured (the dog ran off), and by the time the paramedics arrived, I was walking around, shaking like a leaf. The medics promptly threw a blanket over me, as they had been trained to do with "victims of shock." However, I wasn't in shock, and more than that, I didn't want to stop shaking. So I threw the blanket off. I knew that after a frightening experience I needed to shake and that being warmed by a blanket would hinder this process. I wanted to allow my body to shake until all functions had returned to normal. The medics kept bundling me up, and I kept unbundling myself.

Realizing that I was not going to be allowed to tremble without a fuss, I looked for another form of catharsis. I thought about the poor dog I had hit and it reminded me of all my beloved pets that had been run over. I started to cry. The medics didn't like that any better than the shaking. They must have decided that I was going over the edge, as they got out a hypodermic needle.

I quickly stopped crying before they were able to inject me, but still, even in my disorganized state, I knew that I needed some cathartic release. I began to chat with the medics, lightly and amiably, and to intersperse the conversation with laughter. Laughter was not my body's first or even second choice of catharsis, but the men approved of this behavior and even joined in, which helped them to release their own tensions. This left me to my own devices until my ride came.

The most absurd thing about this accident was that while the medics were earnestly trying to take care of my needs, I had to work just as hard to meet their requirements by postponing my cathartic processes. They thought that by stopping my response to the trauma (shaking and crying), they would stop the hurt. I was willing to go along with them because I didn't want to be drugged, which would have stopped my catharsis entirely. I knew that the painful emotions from this trauma would keep and I would be able to take care of them later. Once again, laughter came to my rescue as an acceptable form of catharsis, and in this case, it helped me release some of the less severe aspects of this event.

CATHARSIS HEALS!

> The effect of laughter upon the mind not only brings relaxation with it, so far as mental tension is concerned, but makes it also less prone to dreads and less solicitous about the future. This favorable effect on the mind influences various functions of the body and makes them healthier than would otherwise be the case.
>
> —*James Walsh, American physician*

Modern medicine's approach is to remove the symptoms of physiological problems and claim healing. By drugging or disallowing catharsis in medical practice, we are cut off from our natural healing process. Most people believe that if we stop someone from crying, we stop them from hurting, when actually the hurt has already happened and crying is the chemical rebalancing that takes place in order to heal it. This is also true of trembling. The contagion of catharsis is extremely threatening to health professionals, who stop others from "catharting" in order to stay in control of their own emotions. This is not to disparage the remarkable achievements of modern medicine or to discount the use of drugs when truly necessary.

Several years ago, Valium was the most prescribed drug in the U.S. Today it is Prozac, and there is strong evidence that more people are addicted to prescription drugs than social drugs. By drugging all pain, we inadvertently cut ourselves off from powerful self-healing. I know that someday we human beings will trust ourselves enough to realize that we have phenomenal healing abilities within our own bodies and will be able to allow our natural cathartic processes to take place.

THE FUNCTION OF ANGER

> If a man can't laugh there is some mistake made in putting him together, and if he won't laugh he wants as much keeping away from as a bear-trap when it is set.
>
> —*Josh Billings*

Anger is a vital emotion. We feel angry when we are treated in an unaware, unconscious way. One of my favorite examples of anger is not in the human category but involves a mother dog. When I was growing up, my family always had female dogs, and often litters of puppies. When the puppies were about three weeks old, they developed little needle teeth and started teething on whatever was available.

I remember puppies finding their mother's ear and chewing on it with great fervor. She would emit a very low growl, so low that the puppies didn't even hear it and kept on chewing. She then escalated her growl, at which time they stopped chewing and looked around, obviously puzzled, to see where the strange noise had come from. Not realizing that the growl was connected to their mother or to what they were doing, they continued to chew. The third time they did this, she really blasted them with a ferocious snap. They dropped her ear and yipped frantically with surprise. She never bit them or harmed them, but she did let them know that they were not to chew on her ear. Needless to say, they never did it again, and they never forgot what a growl was about. She established a firm boundary.

We are all walking around in our lives, unaware that we occasionally chew on each other's ears. This lack of awareness is common to us all. We depend on one another to draw our attention to actions that are off-base. This is where anger comes in. Often, if someone is bothering us, the first time we try to get their attention, they don't even notice. The second time we escalate our efforts, and if that doesn't work, then the third time we really let them have it. This immediate anger is not long or prolonged, nor does it involve physical violence. It merely draws the other person's attention to their behavior so they can stop it.

The reason that we become red-faced, warm, and sweaty with anger is because this sudden outburst requires a massive blood flow for a very short period of time, often only a few seconds. The most common example of this is what we usually refer to as embarrassment. When we are teased or laughed at, very often we will flush, which is an angry response to being humiliated.

THE FEAR-ANGER CONNECTION

> The beauty of the world has two edges; One of laughter, one of anguish, cutting the heart asunder.
>
> —*Virginia Woolf*

Anger is probably one of the most misunderstood emotions. The word anger is used to describe many kinds of human behavior that really have nothing to do with the emotion of anger or rage. As a result, we are confused and at a loss at how to handle certain behaviors.

All of us are aware that fear produces certain chemicals that prepare us for fight or flight. We forget that fighting has to do with fear and assume when people fight they are angry. Actually, they are defending themselves because they are afraid. I believe that all violence (such as throwing things, screaming at people, hitting people, and committing violent crimes) has its source in fear, or perhaps unresolved grief. In documentary prison films where inmates are asked about their emotional states during violent crimes, almost all report that while being violent, they experienced intense fear. There are many more men imprisoned for violent acts than women. Men tend to wear fear more than anger. Men are taught not to admit or show fear. The worst thing that you can say about a man is that he is a "coward," a "sissy," or just plain "yellow." As a result, men are forced into repressing their fear. They act macho, tough, and angry, and slam things around, which produces fear in others. This is harmful to relationships and creates insecurity, resulting in more fear for the macho man. The more fear that is repressed, the more macho the man becomes in order to cover up the fear. The more violent the relationship, the more fear there is, and that fear keeps recycling and compounding. As women, we don't want our men to be afraid because they are supposed to protect and take care of us. We collude with their fear and excuse them for their mislabeled "angry," violent outbursts.

HEART DISEASE AND THE FEAR OF LOSS

> They carried all the emotional baggage of men who might die . . . too frightened to be cowards . . . they died so as not to die from embarrassment.
>
> —*Tim O'Brien*

Years ago, research came up with the Type A personality profile, which was used to predict the onset of heart disease. Characteristics listed as predictors of heart disease included impatience, workaholism, and hostility. Recently this personality profile was retested and only one characteristic held up as a predictor of heart disease: unresolved hostility. I believe the hostility component of heart disease is actually a fear component.

Heart disease seems on the surface to be a failure of the heart. In metaphoric view, this disease could be an indication of the failure of intimacy and loving. More men than women get heart disease and more men than women have problems with intimacy. This seems true because men, more than women, are afraid of loss, simply because they aren't allowed to cry. When someone is not allowed to cry their losses over a long period of time, he will avoid any attachment that might produce further loss. Any new loss might trigger the backlog of tears. For the same reason, men don't laugh as much as women because they know that if they laugh hard enough or long enough they will cry. Rather than loving all-out, men tend to withhold love (or create double messages of "come-close-stay-away") in order to protect themselves from further loss. Men have been trained since childhood (often by their mothers), to repress their tears, and so are unable to cathart and heal themselves through crying.

If the emotion attached to heart disease is fear rather than hostility, that fear may be the fear of loss. Many men who experience loss, or the fear of loss, will act angry. During my marriage, I developed many ailments and illnesses in the process of having three children and trying to be a superwoman. I have a vivid memory of my husband standing over me while I was sick in bed, with fury and anger and rage all over him. I had no way of understanding why he was acting angry at me when I was so sick and needed him to be compassionate and caring. Now I realize that he was terrified of losing me, and in his fear of loss, the only behavior available to him was to act angry.

Unfortunately, the way men have been forced to dramatize their fear and grief (by acting angry), has resulted in our culture's misunderstanding of anger. It would be interesting to run some tests to measure body temperature during so-called "angry" episodes. My guess is that men would test cool in body temperature as opposed to warm, thus indicating fear, not anger.

THE TABOO ON WOMEN AND ANGER

> The important thing in acting is to be able to laugh and cry. If I have to cry, I think of my sex life; if I have to laugh, I think of my sex life.
>
> —*Glenda Jackson*

Women in our culture are not allowed to be angry. The worst thing we can say about a women is that she is "an angry bitch." As women we are supposed to be sweet and kind, compliant, and always say yes. Perhaps the best example of this behavior is our century's most outstanding sex symbol, Marilyn Monroe. It is almost impossible to imagine Marilyn Monroe being angry, really angry. Here is a woman who was horribly abused sexually as a child, who was unable to say no, and was, as an adult, sexually manipulated by countless film and political figures, including possibly a president. She was totally vulnerable, talked like a little girl, and due to her abuse, had no sexual boundaries. To imagine her angry would completely negate her image. She would no longer be sexually appealing. It is a sad commentary on our culture that sex appeal must take this form.

ARTHRITIS AND THE MARTYR SYNDROME

> Co-dependency is just a trendy term for being a well-socialized woman. We're all trained to put other people's needs before our own. We're trained to be validated by what our husbands, children, and lovers think of us. It's not uniquely feminine but it

is considered normal in women, whereas in men it's considered a disease.

—*Erica Jong*

More women than men have arthritis which, unlike heart disease, is considerably less life-threatening. Arthritis is an inflammation of the tissues of the joints or connecting tissues between cells. People who work in the field of arthritis are aware that part of the personality type of arthritic patients is the so-called martyr syndrome. Martyred people have a great deal of unresolved rage, bitterness, resentment, and anger at the bottom of all their self-sacrificing. When they give up so much, there is an expectation (however unconscious) of some kind of return.

As the child of two arthritic parents (my mother suffers from osteoarthritis and my father from rheumatoid arthritis), I know the martyr syndrome well. It was very subtle, but someone in our family was always sacrificing something for someone else (as opposed to no-strings-attached nurturing and caring). My father (who seldom laughed) had a prolonged bout with rheumatoid arthritis, then developed heart disease, had three heart attacks, and died as a result. My mother (who laughs a lot) has suffered from chronic osteoarthritis for as long as I can remember, and she is still alive.

I too became a martyr. For years I carried an invisible portable stake for my Joan of Arc act. Whenever I felt particularly martyred, I would pause, pound my metaphorical stake into the ground, and lash myself to it, reaching down and lighting the fire under my feet. At this point the joints in my feet would begin to throb intensely. The pain would tell me that I had some anger and rage to take care of.

It would usually go something like this: "I gave him such a nice gift for his birthday. You'd think he'd call me. Is it too much to ask for a simple phone call? That's not too much to ask, is it? Anyone would have done that! You would have done that wouldn't you? Of course you would!"

Those of us who have the martyr syndrome always have expectations that are reasonable, but we expect those things of people we have trained not to give to us. Because we are so self-sacrificing with them, they don't have to give. The only way we can be a martyr is to constantly self-sacrifice with no return, so we have to find and train people not to give back to us in any way.

FUEL FOR THE FIRE: RAGE

> I remember one particular weekend when my husband was gone, and I was juggling all the children. I was tired, frazzled, and I had a lot of homework for the next day that I had not yet gotten to. Then the phone rang, and in addition to everything else, I was told I would be interviewing the Vice President. I just started laughing. What else could I do?
>
> —*Jane Pauley*

In this country, women are taught to be self-sacrificing. In my generation, a good mother was someone who gave up her own life for her children. As women, we were encouraged to do this—to put aside our own needs and wants—for the privilege and joy of having children and a husband. Younger women now have the added stress of all the old expectations plus new ones: taking care of their own needs and being a bread winner at the same time as providing emotional and physical support for their families.

Having to "do it all" produces tremendous rage. The rage is at our culture, our husbands and children, and particularly at ourselves for having bought into this expectation. We are taught to expect the support of our husbands, the love of our children, and the appreciation of the culture for our sacrifice. As evidenced by the divorce rate, and by the number of single women with children in poverty, the promise of women being taken care of by men has turned out to be a lie. But women still maintain the façade of pleasantness and sweetness with smiles and soft voices.

I have found that in both men and women, the softer and more controlled the voice, the greater the rage. I have begun to view women, particularly certain women clients of mine, as Madame Peles. Pele is the volcano goddess of Hawaii, and I don't think it is by chance that the volcano is represented by a goddess and not by a god.

Women have a tendency to feel like victims because we don't express our rage. When we are stuck in a victim pattern, we feel powerless to bring about change. Powerlessness and dependency always breed rage. If we as women are dependent on men to take care of us, we become enraged toward them.

RAGE AND LAUGHTER

> There are three ways to get something done; do it yourself, hire someone, or forbid your kids to do it.
>
> —*Monta Crane*

As self-sacrificing mothers, we expect our children to do what we want them to, when we want them to do it, in the way we want them to. When they don't do this, we become enraged. When I first began as a client, participating in the cathartic process of therapy, I got in touch with my enormous rage toward my inability to control my children's behavior. In order to deal with this rage in session, I fantasized the worst possible thing that I could do to my children. I imagined putting each one down the garbage disposal, feet first. Feet first was important, so that I could watch their little faces as they slowly went down the grinder. As I fantasized this, I would laugh the most incredible rage-filled laugh. As a result of this exercise, which I engaged in on more than one occasion, I was able to be much more loving to my children. When they asked me for something, instead of snapping an immediate "no" to them, I was able to be more patient. Instead of my anger leaking out in all the conversations I had with them, I was much softer, and able to be with them in a much more loving and caring way. I have used this technique with many of my clients, and so far, no one has put a real child through a real garbage disposal. Many parent-child relationships have improved and become more loving as a result of using cathartic, angry laughter.

LAUGH YOUR WAY THROUGH CO-DEPENDENCY

> O! Hwai dungsyi—You bad little thing—said the woman, teasing her baby granddaughter. "Is Buddha teaching you to laugh for no reason?" As the baby continued to gurgle, the woman felt a deep wish stirring in her heart.
>
> "Even if I could live forever," she said to the baby, "I still don't know which way I would teach you. I was once so free and innocent. I too laughed for no reason.
>
> "But later I threw away my foolish innocence to protect myself. And then I taught my daughter, your mother, to shed her innocence so she would not be hurt as well.
>
> "Hwai dungsyi, was this kind of thinking wrong? If I now recognize evil in other people, is it not because I have become evil too? If I see someone has a suspicious nose, have I not smelled the same bad things?"
>
> The baby laughed, listening to her grandmother's laments.
>
> "O! O! You say you are laughing because you have already lived forever, over and over again? You say you are Syi Wang Mu Queen Mother of the Western Skies, now come back to give me the answer! Good, good, I am listening . . .
>
> "Thank you, Little Queen. Then you must teach my daughter this same lesson. How to lose your innocence but not your hope. How to laugh forever."
>
> —*Amy Tan*

There is a movement sweeping our country that deals with issues of co-dependency. This movement looks at the damaging ways that people become dependent on one another, and the results of these kinds of relationships. Melody Beattie, in her book *Co-Dependent No More,* defines a co-dependent person as "one who has let another person's behavior affect him or her, and who is obsessed with controlling that person's behavior." This can happen between men and women, parents and children, or friends and relatives. Whole religions can be looked at as co-dependent, as can governments, organizations, and businesses.

In male-female relationships, there is an old, co-dependent notion that two people come together to make a whole, instead of two whole people coming together to make a team. A healthy couple or team directs its attention out into the world, supporting and caring about one another. Each one can then take care of him or herself as they best need to do and go about their work. Partially developed adults who come together in order to complete themselves start out looking deeply into each other's eyes and taking care of each other, then end up glaring at each other with hate.

We as women are classic co-dependents and need to begin to laugh about the seriousness we impose on our situations. Once we begin to laugh that wonderful deep, rich, angry laugh, we will be able to think more clearly about how to resolve our dilemma. We'll stop taking out our anger on our little boys, our husbands, and men in general, and we will feel better about ourselves and probably have less arthritis.

"BORED? NOT ON YOUR LIFE!"

> Boredom is a vital problem for the moralist since at least half the sins of mankind are caused by fear of it.
>
> —*Bertrand Russell*

There are many people who deny that boredom even exists. I would prefer to be in that category, because it is so boring to talk and write about boredom. Author Sven Birkerts in the Boston Phoenix says, "Boredom is America's dirty little secret. At least I suspect it is—since a secret is, by definition, something nobody talks about."

I have noticed that when I mention boredom at my presentations, it is always the object of many questions, with people desperate to discuss it. People seem to fall into two categories regarding boredom. One group admits to their boredom with exasperation, and proceeds to list all their boring moments—everything from work to making love. The other group is more common. They vehemently profess, "I never get bored. I don't understand how anyone could be bored, there's so much to do."

We all experience boredom, and that it is by far the most painful of our emotions. It may create a chemistry in parts of the brain (as opposed to fear and anger, which we experience in our bodies) that results in the experience of a "heavy head," or mental paralysis. Birkerts further reflects:

"I believe boredom is the unacknowledged malaise of our times, with the gravity of the situation compounded by our reluctance to admit that we are bored. People will, statistics inform us, watch more T.V., file more divorces, visit more psychiatrists, buy more nonessential commodities, flock as never before to watch celluloid orgies of sex and bloodshed . . . but admit boredom? Heavens, no!

"When boredom sets in, take solace, at least, in this. Boredom is not trivial, but profound. It is what results when an irresistible force, the juggernaut of unattainable desires, meets an immovable object, the naked truth of how things are. If no crisis existed in former times, it's not because the naked truth was any different. People were simply not worked up to such a level of wanting."

"BOREDOM, TEE-HEE!"

> Some children are born with the ability to think; our schools are designed to cure them of this habit.
>
> —*Bertrand Russell*

As you read this information, you may actually feel bored! I was reluctant to include boredom in this book, because writing and reading about boredom is boring. Any unfinished boredom from the past that has gone unresolved or uncatharted will come to the surface. It is probably for this reason that almost no research has been done on boredom. The research would be excruciatingly boring and painful for the researchers. If you experience boredom while reading this section of the book, it may not be my lack of writing ability, but rather a triggering of your own stored-up boredom. In order to combat this, as I write about boredom, I am going to remind you to stop and say, "Boredom, tee-hee."

I have two definitions for boredom: Boredom results from either (1) too much input, stimulation, or information coming at us, or (2) too little. The best example of this would be school. ("School, tee-hee.") Boredom is rampant in the school system primarily because there is no way a single teacher with forty children in a classroom can tailor the information input for each student. As a result, at any given time, a large number of students in any classroom are experiencing boredom (tee-hee).

THE CASE OF THE BORING WEATHER INSTRUCTOR

> Must you know the reason for everything?
>
> —*Charlie Chaplin*

We have all experienced listening to a speaker who is extraordinarily boring. Years ago when I first moved aboard my boat and was planning my future as a sailor, I realized it would help if I knew something about the weather. Fortunately, the University of California was offering a weekend course on weather, taught by a distinguished weather expert. His biography listed all kinds of supervisory and teaching positions, and appointments to innumerable national and international weatherboards. I was very impressed and felt fortunate to have access to such an outstanding expert for relatively little money.

I went off to the seminar with great expectations. It wasn't long, however, before I realized that this man planned to tell us everything he knew about weather in the space of two days. I also noticed that after each break, fewer people would return. I, however, hung in there until the bitter end, hoping that somehow, someone or something would suddenly transform the tedium into an enlightening ("tee-hee") experience.

By the time the seminar reached its conclusion late Sunday afternoon, there were only eight left out of the original forty people. Evaluation forms for the course were handed out, and I went into great detail (anonymously, of course) about how hard it was for me to stay interested when there was no chance to laugh or be playful with the material. I suggested to the instructor that he do something about his teaching style, and informed him that he was incredibly boring. I spilled this out with great relief and without much censoring, particularly since the evaluations were anonymous.

About a year and a half later I began teaching my laughter classes and, lo and behold, who should show up in my class but this particular weather instructor. I, of course, recognized him. As each person came in front of the group to explain why they were taking the class, he quoted, almost verbatim, the paragraph that I had written on my evaluation. My heart was in my throat, even though I realized that he didn't recognize me.

This is one of the more ironic events of my life, and one of the funniest. The weather expert went on to develop a rather delicious laugh and a twinkling sense of humor, which allowed him, I'm sure, to adopt a new approach for his future presentations. If he is now reading this, I apologize for not 'fessing up.

BOREDOM AND CATHARSIS

> When the voices of children are heard on the green,
> And laughing is heard on the hill,
> My heart is at rest within my breast,
> And everything else is still.
>
> —*William Blake*

Like anger and fear, boredom is an emotion designed to stimulate action. If too much information is coming in, then the action the brain takes is either to shut down so it won't receive the information, or better still, to propel us to leave the scene or to take some other action that will lessen the information input.

One cathartic resolution for the chemistry of boredom is a certain kind of laughter. The body temperature is normal and the laughter sounds delightful. It is lyrical and musical—a wonderful laugh to be around. When I work with clients on boredom, it is often easy for them to laugh merely by describing the boring situation. The desire for the human organism not to be bored is so great that laughter comes very easily. Unfortunately, when we find ourselves trapped in boring situations, laughter is probably the least acceptable behavior and must be taken care of later.

The other resolution for boredom is talking, and there are two kinds. The first kind is excited talking. Most of us have had the experience, either as a parent or caregiver, of having a child come home from a movie and begin to relate to us all the details of the events they witnessed. I particularly remember my son doing this when he was about six or seven. He would go on and on and on, pausing only to take a deep breath now and then. I would lay in wait for these pauses and try, in a nice way, to end this harangue of boring details because I was so excruciatingly bored. I know that his talking was a release of boredom because I was so bored listening to it. That is an example of the contagion of catharsis.

The other kind of talking is reluctant talking. Reluctant talking stems from being at a boring event where there is too little stimulation, as opposed to the previous example where too much stimulation results in excited talking. I'm sure we've all had the experience of asking a friend how a lecture or movie or play was and got as a response a groan or an "Oh, well," or "Gosh, it was okay." Most of us won't leave it at that and we prod on, asking our friend for more details, once again receiving very vague, hesitant, and stilted replies. Usually this persistence results in a change of subject, or we just give up.

I like to think of laughter as being a very efficient form of catharsis. It takes care of three of our painful emotions (at least the lighter levels of those emotions): boredom, fear, and anger. The only thing laughter cannot rebalance chemically is grief, which must be resolved through tears. As I have said in this chapter, each of these laughs sounds different and has a different body temperature, as well as producing different chemicals in the body. That is why I like to think of laughter as the most effective form of catharsis. Even if laughter didn't do all of these things, it sure gives us a enjoyable way out of feeling bad.

CHAPTER 8

Laugh Your Way to You

> The sound of laughter is like the vaulted dome of a temple of happiness.
>
> —*Milan Kundera*

To wind up all this information on laughter, I think it might be helpful to reflect on some of laughter's broader effects. I have written about the physiology of laughter, and I do believe laughter has profound, precise, and measurable effects on our bodies, as well as our minds, emotions, and spirits.

In spite of those measurable effects, our society still views laughter as something ethereal, a sound floating through the airwaves, pleasant to experience but not really of major significance. We have a vested interest in downplaying the power of laughter. Culture "cultivates" society by setting standards—which in turn become rigid expectations of behavior. These expectations do not consider individual needs, and the result is tremendous tension. Faced by the "shoulds" of our families and culture, we learn early on to hide our authentic selves.

WHO ARE WE?

> Dance, my heart! dance today with joy. The strains of love fill the days and nights with music, and the world is listening to its melodies. Mad with joy, life and death dance to the rhythm of this music.
>
> The hills and the sea and the earth dance. The world of man dances in laughter and tears.
>
> *Songs of Kabir translated by Rabindranath Tagore*

What do I mean by authentic self? I mean those parts of us that dream irrationally, imagine outrageous possibilities, and invent and create intuitively. In addition, we hide our mistakes, desires, needs, and emotions, fearful of being judged wrong, sick, needy, or crazy. By hiding the reality of who we really are, we abandon our authentic selves.

Although we laughed consistently and regularly in my family, there was an unspoken rule not to cry or show anger, fear, or doubt. I remember crying silently into my teddy bear's stomach many, many nights. My family looked so good from the outside. We were so well trained to maintain the illusion of a happy, good family that it has taken me many years of therapy to begin to acknowledge the pain that was so rampant and so repressed. The laughter that happened at dinner every evening was the release valve that kept us from killing ourselves or each other. To cry or show anger would have so transgressed on the unwritten family rule, that doing so would have been to risk harsh judgment, resulting in rejection. Fear of judgment from the outside keeps us behaving in the way the judges have decided. It doesn't take long to internalize the process into self-judgment.

DO YOU "SHOULD" ON YOURSELF?

> There are only three eternal elements in the world. God, Human folly, and laughter. And since the first two pass all comprehension, we must do what we can with the third.
>
> —*Old Arab Saying*

"Feeling guilty" is actually pain that results from our harsh judgment of ourselves and others based on what we think we or others should or should not do. When we "should" on ourselves, it hurts. Guilt-tripping is nearly always inflicted deliberately. Yet the pain of guilt is what we have chosen to divert us from our primal pain: we sell out to the "shoulds" and abandon our authentic selves in order to survive our childhoods.

Guilt gives us the illusion of being in control of our primal pain. The desperate avoidance of our primal pain stems from our fear of being powerless: if we face the pain and the loss of our authentic selves, we are afraid it will be like jumping into a flood-swollen river and being swept away. Guilt, although excruciatingly painful, seems at least manageable. We believe we can turn it on and off at will because it is self-inflicted. What happens, however, is that the pain takes over, and our clear thinking, which is the basis of choice, shuts down.

In the absence of being able to make a choice, we become addicted to the predictability of the pain of guilt. Then the more terrifying choice and risk-taking become.

Guilt's illusion of control gives us a false sense of power. Most people believe power is achieved by domination or manipulation—but real power is found in self-confidence. When we acknowledge our feelings, and honor them through communication, expression, and catharsis, we remain true to our authentic selves. Unfortunately, most of us are carrying around old, leftover feelings from our childhood. If we can rebalance and release these stored-up chemical feelings through cathartic action—such as laughter and tears—we can regain our personal power and be less vulnerable to outside power trips.

HOW TO BE A MILLIONAIRE

> Conform and be dull.
>
> —*James Dobie*
>
> The great artists of the world are never Puritans,
> and seldom even ordinarily respectable.
>
> —*H.L. Mencken*

To be our authentic selves means to take risks, to buck the cultural tide, and to lose control of having a guaranteed, secure, predictable future. Paradoxically, some of the people our culture rewards most visibly with massive amounts of money are the artists who flaunt our institutions. The artists making the most money are rock stars and comedians (not to mention dead painters). Rock stars are outrageous: Madonna flaunts sex and religion and rakes in millions, Michael Jackson confuses our notion of sexual identity. They share their rebellion against the "shoulds," and we can vicariously join in, and heap rewards upon them.

Comedians provide us with an acceptable way of losing control—laughter! Bill Cosby helps us laugh about family situations. Other comedians rely on the number-one tension-laden topic: sex. Sex is an excellent example of the gap between what should happen and what really does happen. This is always a guaranteed laugh. (Although Eskimos have hundreds of words to describe snow, they use only one word for both sex and laughter!)

Rock and roll and comedy are dynamic—in direct contrast to our culture's static, predictable mass behavior. Rock stars move us physically, through music; comedians move us emotionally, through laughter. We treasure and reward them for their unpredictability.

Oprah Winfrey, another high-paid entertainer, earns her millions by exposing the truth of our lives and being her authentic self. The popularity of this kind of entertainment (radio call-in and TV talk shows) is a reflection of the hunger that our population feels for authenticity.

LOVE YOUR MOTHER!

> If the world, even for twenty-four hours, decided
> to laugh at everything . . . it will be such a deep
> cleansing phenomenon, it will clean away all dirt.
>
> —*Bhagwan Shree Rajneesh*

If we lived authentically, our lives would be dynamic and always changing, like life in nature. Native American and Eastern cultures revere and respect nature as teacher and as the source of sustenance. In the West we refer to our planet as Mother Earth, but we treat "her" with the same blame and anger we so frequently bestow on our mothers. This may be the basis of our environmental crisis. We expect our mothers to take care of all our needs, be there for us (no matter what is going on with her), to have no life of her own, and to pick up our dirty socks!

Western culture, with its Judeo-Christian roots, has sought to control nature and our human lives. Rather than adapt to our environment, we have adapted the environment to our needs because we are afraid of nature's dynamism. Our Puritan heritage encourages us to control our sensuousness, and thus our pain and pleasure. In our attempts to create a safe, static, controlled environment, we have also tried to control catharsis, particularly laughter. But by its very nature laughter is dynamic, and the epitome of the loss of control.

THE DYNAMIC DUO: LAUGHTER AND RISK-TAKING

> At the height of laughter the universe is flung into a kaleidoscope of new possibilities.
>
> —*Jean Houston*

When we laugh as we need to rather than at specifically approved times, our bodies, emotions, minds, and spirits all move with dynamic energy. We cannot remain stuck. Our thoughts, greased for spontaneity by laughter, create a more flexible being. Laughing readily, the way we did as children, helps us regain self-confidence—which is another way of saying that we reclaim our personal power. Each time we laugh readily, we reinstate a portion of our authentic selves. The more in touch we are with our authentic selves, the more creative we become in the art of living. Most of us tend to avoid taking the risk of discovering who we really are; laughter dispels this fear.

People often comment on the risks I take on stage with laughter, and on my nerviness as a pioneer in laughter therapy long before laughter was officially linked with healing. My ability to take significant risks in public comes from my previous career and training as a painter. In order to be considered a good painter in our culture, you must be demonstrably nuts. I found painting a perfect foundation for being a laughter therapist, with its daily doses of risk-taking, loss of control, and dynamic uncertainty.

EVEN OIL TANKERS CAN BE FUN!

> High comedy, and the laughter that ensues, is an evolutionary event.
>
> —*Jean Houston*

My model in nature for a dynamic, playful, laughing being is the dolphin. I may be projecting laughter onto this creature, but it seems to wear an evolved permanent smile. I have heard it said that a dolphin's brain is larger than ours, and that the dolphin is the most highly adapted creature in nature. Over the years I have collected photographs and posters of dolphins, which remind me of what my true nature could be. One poster depicts seven dolphins bodysurfing a wave just off the beach. Another shows a dolphin playfully leaping in the forward wake of a monstrous oil tanker, which is bearing down menacingly through the sea.

This image speaks to me so deeply that it seems to symbolize my dream of how the world can be for humans. What if we could play and laugh with those things in our world that are so frightening, powerful, and oppressive? There is certainly nothing funny about an oil tanker moving full speed ahead; yet this relatively tiny mammal takes the opportunity to enjoy the bow wake created by the monster's movement.

ALL IS PLAY

> *Cosmic Laugh*
>
> Lifeha/deathha/joyha/sadha/mamaha/ papaha/
> youha/ weha/ theyha./ Come to think of/ it/all
> is Haha.
>
> —*Anonymous*

If we can use laughter more often, we can start to enjoy more of our lives. When we feel good, we care more carefully, think more thoughtfully, sense more sensibly, and act more artfully. Life becomes an opportunity to experience ourselves as we are, to play with our pleasure and pain . . . and to heal ourselves by laughing about everything in our lives that isn't really funny.

> If you are going to be miserable, you might as well enjoy it.
>
> —*Annette Goodheart*

PART TWO

Twenty-five Ways to Help Yourself Laugh

"Strange when you come to think of it, that of all the countless folk who have lived before our time on the planet, not one is known in history or in legend as having died of laughter."

—*Sir Max Beerbohm*

Twenty-five Ways to Help Yourself Laugh

> We must laugh before we are happy, for fear we die before we laugh at all.
>
> —*Jean de Bruyère*

> It's never too late to do nothing at all.
>
> —*Allen Ginsberg*

1. Fake It Till You Make It

"Laughter?" asked Milan Kunder once. "Does anyone ever care about laughter? I mean real laughter—beyond joking, jeering, ridicule. Laughter—delight unbounded, delight delectable, delight of delights."

> I said to my sister or she said to me, come let's play together. We stretched out side by side on the bed and started in. At first we just made believe, of course. Forced laughs. Laughable laughs. Laughs so laughable they made us laugh. Then it came—real laughter, total laughter—sweeping us off in unbounded effusion. Bursts of laughter, laughter rehashed, jostled laughter, laughter defleshed, magnificent laughter, sumptuous and wild . . . And we laughed to the infinity of laughter of our laughs . . . O laughter! Laughter of delight, delight of laughter. Laughing deeply is living deeply.
>
> —*Annie Leclerc*

Faking it is the most obvious way to start laughing when nothing is funny—and yet for some people it's the hardest. No one wants to be accused of a phony laugh. So at first you'll feel self-conscious, forcing it.

Once you get some convulsions going in your diaphragm, your body will take over. You'll be doing it naturally, and maybe remembering things that *are* laughable. Even if the laughter remains mechanical, it will lift your facial muscles into the laughing posture and stimulate your thymus gland. It will remind you of what it's like—how easy it is, after all—to laugh.

The Zen Buddhists who begin each day with fifteen minutes of laughter may have to start by faking it. It's like starting your car on a cold morning: once the ignition turns over, your engine catches. This works because our diaphragms are stupid and cannot distinguish between fake and real laughter.

If you're having difficulty, try it in front of a mirror. The sight of your earnest, quizzical face might be enough to inspire you. Or sit down with a friend and fake it together, thereby doubling your chances of success.

2. Smile More

> I live in a constant endeavor to fence against the infirmities of ill health, and other evils of life, by mirth; being firmly persuaded that every time a man smiles, but much more so, when he laughs, that it adds something to this fragment of life.
>
> —*Laurence Stesne*

If you find it difficult to laugh, then you might want to consider smiling more. If your face is in an "up" position, there is less gravity to fight and laughter will come more easily. In this case, function follows form.

3. Share Your Embarrassing Moments

> I don't make jokes. I just watch the government and report the facts.
>
> —*Will Rogers*

Besides the gift of free laughter, my mother gave me the gift of sharing embarrassing moments. Not a day went by that she didn't tell some story on herself, something that revealed that she was human and had goofed. I recently visited her in Phoenix. As we were driving to lunch, a desert thunderstorm came and went, leaving large droplets on the windshield. Suddenly the sun appeared, and I heard my mother laughing. When I looked over, she explained that she had been brushing spots off her slacks, when she realized that she was trying to brush off the shadows of the raindrops. She laughed again and I was able to join in.

There was really no need for my mother to reveal that she had mistaken shadows for spots on her slacks. She could have kept it to herself and maybe even put herself down for being so stupid and not realizing the difference. Many of us do this and swallow our embarrassment. But she chose to share her experience and laugh again, so we could both share our combined embarrassment over all the times that we have goofed.

Sharing our embarrassing moments allows us to experience connection. By retelling these embarrassing incidents we get back in touch with the pain of the embarrassment that has more often than not gone unreleased. In addition, the listener can also remember unreleased embarrassment and share in the laughter release. This creates a closeness that allows us to see one another as we really are—imperfect, stumbling, bumbling mistake-making human beings.

Share the time you spilled the cup of coffee on your guest's lap, the time you put a letter in a wrong envelope (and sent a love letter to your insurance company), the time when you fell on your face, the time when you were trying to look especially good and discovered that you had your sweater wrong side out, and the time you walked through the restaurant with a piece of toilet paper stuck to your heel. These are the stories we need to share with one another.

I've heard it said that the most successful people are those who have made the most mistakes, and I agree. But I would add: ". . . those who have made the most mistakes and shared them." *Only through open expression can we free ourselves of the pain of humiliation and move on.*

Most embarrassing moments have to do with people getting caught in their postures, pretenses, and poses. We all walk around in our daily lives acting and *looking* like we have it all together. We pretend we have no problems, as if we know exactly where we're going and what we're doing. Then, once in a while, we get tripped up. We get caught with our slip showing or our fly unzipped.

One of my favorite examples of the embarrassing moment was described by a student in one of my laughter classes. Janis was hiking up a narrow, steep canyon trail when she noticed a wildflower growing out of a rock high above her. Believing that this miracle of nature deserved homage, she scrambled up the jagged rocks. When she finally reached the flower and bent over to smell it, all the petals fell off. Foiled in her attempt to make the grand gesture, she laughed and her laughter echoed through the canyon. Nature had played a cosmic Chaplinesque joke on her.

An actor friend of mine, living in New York City, told me that he was eating his sack lunch out on the patio of Lincoln Center where they were doing some construction work. He saw a man winding his way through the ripped-up pavement. The man stumbled and barely caught himself. As he straightened up, he turned around to see who had witnessed this, and when he caught my friend's eye he lifted his hands, shrugged his shoulders, and laughed. It was Rudolph Nureyev.

When you can do the same—when you can openly share your own blunders with others—then you are making an immediate connection with *their* sense of vulnerability. You are appealing directly to their humanity by sharing the release of embarrassed laughter and as a result, you will end up feeling closer.

One reminder: when you tell a story on yourself, do it without putting yourself down. If you say, "Oh, what a jerk I am!" the resulting laughter won't release the tension from the incident, but instead will be releasing the pain you inflicted on yourself by putting yourself down. Just remember that to feel foolish is universal and divine.

4. Laugh Along With Strangers

> Always laugh when you can. It is cheap medicine.
>
> —*Lord Byron*

If you are laughing by yourself alone in a public place, be careful—they may come to take you away. Even at a party, you are not supposed to stand off in a corner by yourself laughing. So it's safer, and therefore easier, to laugh with somebody else who's already laughing.

If I'm rolling my shopping cart through the supermarket and come upon a couple of other shoppers laughing over the carrots, I simply pause for a few moments and join in. I am not laughing about what *they're* laughing about, but they don't seem to mind.

Take every opportunity to laugh.

In one of my groups, after cautioning people not to walk down the main street laughing by themselves, someone eagerly put up his hand and said that he had figured out a way to do this safely. He said that he took the earphones from his Walkman and put them on, tucking the end into his pocket. As he walked down the street laughing, everyone thought that it was because of the tape he was listening to. There *are* creative solutions to *all* sticky problems and I think this is one of the better ones.

5. Collect Toys

> Where playing is not possible then the work done by the therapist is directed toward bringing the patient from a state of not being able to play into a state of being able to play.
>
> —*D.W. Winnicott*

Children don't need toys. They can be content for hours playing with a cardboard box. Adults need toys. Adult toys are usually expensive, which makes them *very* serious. We have cameras, food processors, sports cars, microwaves, stereo systems, VCRs, computers, sailboats, and $200 tennis rackets. We justify these indulgences in the name of recreation, exercise, entertainment, and fun. If our sports car is scratched, we become distressed. We take our family out on the sailboat and scream commands. If we double fault on the tennis court, we throw our $200 tennis racket across the net at our opponent. I have noticed that people often become more tense as a result of their involvement in so-called pleasurable activities.

I recommend that adults go to the toy store and buy themselves some *real* toys. Real toys have *no meaning* and *no redeeming social value*. They are purposeless in that they have no other reason for existing except to provide enjoyment.

Over the years I have collected a number of wind-up toys that I bring along to workshops, conferences, and meetings. There is a dignified penguin who waddles across tabletops, cars that zip around in circles, airplanes that do somersaults, a jumping frog, a pecking myna bird, a crazy little mouse, and a pair of wind-up tennis shoes that march off the edge of a desk and fall to the floor, still marching.

Several years ago I was a presenter at a conference on racism. It was a multiracial gathering, of course, and there was a considerable amount of tension in the air. As I was being seriously and somewhat pompously introduced, I pulled three wind-up penguins out of my purse and set them loose across the stage. After the initial astonishment, all the tension dissolved into laughter. The laughter allowed us to think clearly, connect, and get to the work at hand.

I suggest that people take toys to work. If you're worried about being caught playing with them, just leave them on your desk. I guarantee that sooner or later your co-workers will pause at your desk and start winding up the toys. It's hard not to laugh when a pair of tennis shoes is walking across your desk. Some people think that if office workers are laughing they are not being productive. In fact, work done when people are tense is likely to be less accurate. Toys help relieve tension, which then results in higher productivity and more efficiency.

One workshop that I led recently was attended by a city manager. I later had the opportunity to see him again, and he told me that as a result of my workshop he kept an array of wind-up toys on his desk. When his mayor came in to consult with him, they wound up the toys and laughed for five minutes.

He said they were both aware of the improvement in their meetings.

I should warn you that if you need to maintain your dignity, this suggestion is not for you. Toys give us a vacation from dignity. They permit us to laugh about nothing. Stop in at a toy store and wind up the toys. When I first started doing this, I didn't want to admit to the salesperson that I was doing this for me. I used to say I was looking for a child's gift. Now I have no reservations about announcing that I am looking for toys for myself. It has taken me several years to get to this point.

Something else you can do in a toy store is to ask the salespeople what their favorite toys are. People who work in toy stores get paid close to minimum wage and, because they enjoy working there so much, they will take less money just to be there. When I ask this question, they gleefully take me around the store, showing me their favorite toys, winding them up, pushing the buttons and playing with them. We, of course, laugh. This is how I have found some of my best toys.

A set of jacks is another toy that fits easily into a briefcase or purse. During Laughter and Learning workshops for teachers at the University of California, I promoted their laughter by playing jacks during the breaks. People love to be reminded that they have permission to indulge in such nonsense. The same goes for jumping rope: carry one along with you so that you and your friends can jump together. Say some of those marvelous jumping-rope rhymes from your childhood. Jumping rope was primarily a female activity when I was young. I have found that men also enjoy the jumping and the rhymes. If jumping rope for laughter and fun is not acceptable, you can always say that you're exercising your cardiovascular system.

Another effective laugh-inducer is the ball attached to a paddle with a long rubber band. Sometimes when I'm standing in line—at the movies, at the airport, or at the bank—I take out the paddle and bat the little ball up and down. At first people laugh *at* me. But then someone usually sidles up and says, "Gee, I haven't played with one of those since I was a kid! Would you mind if I tried it?" This starts a demand for my ball and paddle and suddenly there is conversation, playfulness, and laughter in a group of strangers.

6. Play with Small Animals (And Large Ones If You're Brave)

> Hey diddle diddle
> The cat and the fiddle
> The cow jumped over the moon
> The little dog laughed
> To see such sport
> And the dish ran away with the spoon.
>
> —*Mother Goose*

Puppies and kittens will help you laugh without effort. Have you ever stretched out on the floor and let a litter of month-old puppies walk all over you, or chew at your fingers? Puppies attack with love, and laughter is inevitable.

When my children were young we had a basset hound named Brünhilde. When I looked at that dog, she always looked more depressed than I was, and I laughed. She was so droopy and mournful that my spirits would always be lifted.

Studies have shown that animals have a noticeable impact on people's moods and physical states. Pets have been introduced into retirement and convalescent homes with marked improvement in the residents' blood pressure. Playing with small animals is a loving and entertaining way to bring more laughter into our lives.

Playing with large animals is certainly a bigger risk than playing with small animals, but it can result in bigger laughs. Perhaps my biggest laugh playing with a large animal happened some years ago at Sea World, when they still had a petting pool. At that time, there was a rather large population of dolphins and pilot whales, and one baby orca (or killer whale). As I stood leaning precariously over the edge of the pool, I struck up a close relationship with the young orca. Having just seen the killer whale show, I was aware that these animals love to have their tongues scratched. I found myself with my arm in this creature's mouth, scratching its tongue. Needless to say, a crowd gathered thinking that I was a trainer of some sort. I couldn't take my eyes off the teeth of this obviously carnivorous creature, but when it closed its jaw on my arm, my arm was able to occupy the area at the tip of its mouth where there are no teeth. The orca would pull gently on my arm with several tugs and I would gently pull its tongue back.

We did this for what seemed like a very long time, until the crowd laughed suddenly. When I broke my focus on the tongue tug-of-war and looked to my right, there was a dolphin sitting on its tail about two feet away from my face, its mouth wide open, making that incredible laughing sound that dolphins do so well. I jumped, releasing the tongue of the orca in complete surprise, and, of course, was then able to join in the laughter with the crowd and the dolphin. I have always cherished this memory of playing with larger animals, not only for being able to laugh with an orca, but also for having been laughed at by a dolphin.

7. Make a "Serious" List and Be Very, Very Serious About It

> Boswell: "So, Sir, you laugh at schemes of political improvement?"
> Johnson: "Why, Sir, most schemes of political improvement are very laughable things."
> —*Samuel Johnson*

Making a "serious" list has two benefits. First, if you do it conscientiously, you'll see how much of your daily life consists of stressful pursuits. Second, once you look at this very serious list, you're bound to achieve the perspective that allows you to laugh.

At a recent workshop, a woman said she needed to work on the seriousness of her separation and impending divorce. I asked her to tell us about the seriousness of separation and divorce. Whenever she said "Separation and divorce are very serious," she laughed. But when she focused on her feelings about her marital status, she was able to step back from the actual situation. The resulting perspective allowed her to release the tension through laughter.

After you make your list, read it to yourself or in front of a mirror, very seriously. Frown and say to yourself, "My job is very serious business. My finances are very serious. My family is very very serious. . . ."

Seriousness, which passes for concern, importance, and responsibility, is the way we control our emotions. We clamp our faces into a serious expression, our voices into a serious monotone, and our bodies into a rigid posture in order to not express or reveal our fear, anger, or grief.

When I made my first serious list, I finally was able to laugh about all kinds of things in my life that had been weighing very heavily on me. As I became able to scratch each one off, my life became lighter and lighter. The item that was most resistant and difficult to laugh about was the one I entitled "men." When I was finally able to laugh about "men," my relationships began to change and the seriousness I had imposed on all male friendships and romances began to melt away and transform. In making my current serious list, these are the things I've come up with that I need to laugh about.

1. My brother
2. My sister
3. My mother
4. My ex-husband
5. My knee
6. My weight
7. My anger
8. My book writing
9. Being 59
10. Being serious about laughter

8. Laugh With a Baby

> When the first baby laughed for the first time, the laugh broke into a thousand pieces and they all went skipping about, and that was the beginning of fairies.
>
> —*from* Peter Pan, *by Sir James Matthew Barrie*

Children aged four laugh once every four minutes, which averages out to about 500 times per day. Younger children laugh at least that much, or even more. Whenever I see a baby, I make a special effort to go over and make eye contact. I've learned that it's difficult to maintain seriousness around babies.

We tolerate making faces and silly noises if they are directed at a baby. You can make yourself laugh by attempting to entertain or catch a baby's attention. Very often the baby will laugh along with you, or sometimes they will stare at you as if you are crazy.

If you are with a baby, try the game of peek-a-boo (now I'm here, now I'm not). It not only allows you to be playful and laugh, but the baby will be able to release light fear concerning the disappearance of adults.

After making faces and talking baby-talk with the baby, I often do the same with the parent and we all laugh.

9. Do Something Out of Character

> Against the assault of laughter—nothing can stand.
>
> —*Mark Twain*

When I was a child, my parents often had dinner parties where the best china and silver were set out on white linen. In the middle of dinner my father might say, stiffly, to my mother: "Helen, would you please pass the rolls?" She would pick one out of the basket and deftly fling it across the table—and he would catch it with perfect aplomb. They did this on more than one occasion and I remember the laughter that resulted. The formal evening's tension was exploded.

My father, though a very serious person, also had a musical side. In fact, he kept his Sousaphone, a large tuba-like instrument, on a stand in the corner of the dining room and every once in a while, when he was in a particularly good mood, he would take the Sousaphone down off its roost and proceed to bounce around the house playing this incredibly large brass instrument. I clearly remember fine white powder sifting down from the ceiling as he would scrape against it with the horn. Our dog would run behind the couch and howl, as the rest of the family laughed uproariously.

When we do something out of character, it often results in

laughter. This gives everyone present an opportunity to laugh and join in the fun of the incongruity.

So the next time you're at a gathering—whether it's a party, meeting, or luncheon—take a chance. Maintain an otherwise dignified manner, but do something that's unexpected.

10. Tell Someone What You Laughed About

> The most wasted day of all is that in which we have not laughed.
>
> —*Sebastian Roch Nicolas Chamfort*

During the eleven years that I taught my laughter classes, we always spent the first hour sharing what each of us laughed about during the previous week. There were some specific guidelines about this exercise: the stories had to be from each person's personal experience, not from T.V., a joke, or a movie; and the story could not contain ridicule or teasing.

As people told their stories several delightful things occurred. First, the storyteller learned to speak in front of a group about personal subjects, and to laugh again in the retelling. Second, many of the listeners also laughed, sharing in the process. Third, we were reminded not only of similar laughable events in our own lives, but also how many laughable events do exist!

11. Help Somebody Else Laugh

> Among those whom I like, I can find no common denominator, but among those whom I love, I can: all of them make me laugh.
>
> —*W.H. Auden*

You probably remember what causes your spouse, your children, and your best friends to laugh.

If you notice that one of your children laughed about a riddle the other day, have the child repeat the riddle. Chances are laughter will occur again and you can join in. If you remember a funny story your spouse told you, ask your spouse to tell it to you again and join in with the laughter.

Helping people laugh is very different from *making* people laugh. When we *help* people laugh, we have already observed what they can laugh about and consider laughable. By having them repeat it, they will laugh again. When we *make* people laugh, we are controlling what they will laugh about. It is insensitive to assume that others need to laugh. Very often, the truth is that *we* need to laugh, and we try to get others to laugh so we can join in. By helping people laugh instead of making them laugh, we assure we don't tread on any toes, hurt any feelings, or act insensitive to their needs.

12. Have a Family Reunion With or Without Your Family

> Laughter is the shortest distance between two people.
>
> —*Victor Borge*

A woman in one of my laughter classes once told the class that she and her sister shared long-distance laughing phone calls. She told us that she and her sister had always laughed a lot together and now even though they live many miles apart, they continue the tradition.

Getting together with members of our family is a wonderful opportunity to retell the stories that always bring laughter. Every family has a history, and it usually includes embarrassing moments or minor disasters. Often these stories center on holidays, weddings, or other major events. Sometimes they are as simple as this one from my family.

My brother loved cherry pie, and my mother made cherry pies that were unequaled. She always put them out on the back porch to cool. One night at dinner, my brother, unable to wait any longer, begged to bring in the pie. When he returned, his face was collapsed with despair. He had dropped the cherry pie upside down on the back porch. This event was not funny at the time, but as the years passed, all we had to say was "cherry pie" and the whole family would laugh.

Old photograph albums and old home movies often lead to laughter. It is difficult for visitors to appreciate these family relics, but for the family itself, they often trigger poignant and funny stories. One of my favorite family photographs is of my sister at age four obviously needing to go to the bathroom. She is caught in the act of restraining herself right there in the family album. Every time I look at this picture, I laugh, without the risk of embarrassing her!

13. Imagine John Hancock . . . .

> Laughter need not be cut out of anything, since it improves everything.
>
> —*James Thurber*

The act of putting pen to paper is often performed solemnly. This is an area that could stand some laughter. Fortunately, there are suitable ball-point pens available. They are shaped like fruits, vegetables, fish, ice cream cones, and toothpaste tubes. I recommend that you keep several of these pens handy for signing checks, contracts, loan applications, and insurance policies.

I had an experience with Mexican customs in which my pen played an important role. Many years ago I smuggled a small plant into the United States and have felt guilty ever since. When I go through Mexican customs, I have a horror of being discovered, thrown into jail, and forgotten forever. This old fear clutches my heart and dampens my palms every time I find myself at the border. One time I pulled out my carrot pen to sign my tourist card and the official started laughing. I was as startled by his laughter as he was by my pen. He ran down the hall and brought his superior out of his office to see my pen. The entire customs staff was soon gathered around and we all laughed together.

One of my clients is a lawyer who works exclusively in probate. It bothered him that people were so serious when they came into his office to sign their wills. He understood that nobody enjoys preparing to die, but he wanted to change the mood. For everyone's sake, he bought a set of vegetable pens and left them out on his desk. He has told me that laughing out loud is still rare, but the pens have provoked a few smiles. Imagine John Hancock signing the Declaration of Independence with an asparagus pen!

14. Do A Winking Meditation

> When the highest type of men hear Tao,
> They diligently practice it.
> When the average type of men hear Tao,
> They half believe in it.
> When the lowest type of men hear Tao,
> They laugh heartily at it.
> If they did not laugh at it, it would not be Tao.
>
> —*Lao Tsu*

This is a practice that I often recommend for people who are involved in one of the new-age spiritual movements, and who take their meditation exercises seriously. It can, however, be used by anyone.

Do this with a like-minded friend: Sit on the floor in your meditation posture and look deeply into one another's eyes. Let your highest thoughts, your most cherished mantras come into your mind. Sit there, looking into each other's eyes lovingly and meaningfully.

Then close one eye. And open it again.

Close it . . . and open it, picking up speed, until the other person catches on. Winking at one another nearly always produces laughter and has become a lost art in need of revival.

Add winking to your daily practices and you'll be giving your spirit the breath of fresh air that it needs.

A recent episode of the PBS television series "All Creatures Great and Small" featured a winking cow. The children would gather around this cow and laugh uproariously. It was finally entered in a contest to determine the best cow in the region and won because it winked at the judges.

15. Say, "Seriously . . . "

> The jester is brother to the sage.
>
> —*Arthur Koestler*

This is the oldest trick in the book for comedians. It always means the opposite. We are so conditioned to hearing the word "seriously" used in this way that it automatically triggers a smile.

Try it. Stand in front of a mirror and say, "Seriously now . . ." The corners of your mouth will turn up despite themselves. You get a free smile out of it.

On an individual level, most of us have private catch-phrases that, when shared with certain friends, will trigger laughter. An airplane test pilot, for example, told me that he and his buddy, also a flier, had a private joke around the words "and that's not funny!" It began when one of them suffered a near-fatal crash, and it became the term they used to express their fear. It was their mechanism for handling the enormous stress of their jobs. When the test pilot discovered that he had cancer, he broke the news to his friend and afterward said, "Yeah, Bill . . . and that's not funny!"

16. Throw A Unique Party

> Come live and be merry and you join with me
> To sing the sweet chorus of Ha Ha Hee.
>
> —*William Blake*

Slumber parties are a wonderful tribal ritual—and there's no reason to restrict them to girls or the young. We can all afford to step out of our adult clothes and into our jammies for one evening and revert to a less serious age. We need to lighten up, tell secrets, and giggle.

Giggling is what slumber parties are all about. I remember sitting with my friends in our pajamas, talking and laughing, eating popcorn and laughing and laughing and laughing and laughing and laughing. At some point, usually around three in the morning, the father of the house came into the room to quiet us down. After he left, for a few seconds, it was absolutely silent. Then the giggles burst out again.

If you're serious about wanting to laugh, organize a slumber party for a few of your friends. I went to one recently. There were about a dozen women there, ranging in age from late twenties to mid-fifties. We moved the furniture out of the living room and put our sleeping bags on the floor, with our teddy bears. We indulged in goodies from the delicatessen and then spent the rest of the night telling our most outrageous stories. We giggled ourselves to sleep.

If you are a male, slumber parties might not be a part of your heritage. Instead, you and your boyhood buddies probably had farting contests. I remember when I would haul my sons and six or seven of their friends to the movies in the back of my station wagon. They got into farting and giggling and, of course, I didn't understand what it was all about and I didn't know what to do. I just pretended that I didn't notice and drove as fast as I could so I could unload my charges as quickly as possible. So if you're a man, you might want to get together with a few of your old friends and revert. I do, however, recommend slumber parties for either sex.

There are other kinds of parties you can design. One of the best parties that I ever attended was a very creative approach to helping people get to know one another. We were told to bring finger food (that could be eaten without utensils). When we arrived, we all received a bib. The food was set out on a table and the instructions were that we had to feed one another without speaking. We could make noises, but were asked not to speak. It's hard not to feel close to someone when you have your fingers in her mouth and her sustenance for the evening is dependent upon you and your willingness to feed her. When we dispensed with verbal communication, we were able to laugh freely and for long periods of time, which meant that the dinner went on for several hours. Talk is very often the thing that keeps us from laughing.

For another kind of party, invite ten or twelve of your friends over after dinner. Don't serve any food or drinks as a distraction, and don't tell them this ahead of time. When they arrive, inform them that it is going to be an evening of sharing embarrassing moments. You may need to share first in order to get the ball rolling. Once the ice has been broken with the first story, people will be eager to join in with their own stories. As a result of this kind of sharing, your friends will laugh more and leave your house knowing each other better and feeling closer to one another.

17. Seek Out People Who Laugh

> The number-one reason for choosing a mate is the ability to laugh together.
>
> —*Parade magazine poll, 1985*

You might be surprised to discover that the people you spend the most time with are those with whom you laugh the least. We are told that marriage is a very serious business, and so we marry people with whom we seldom laugh. When we interview for jobs, we tend to focus on duties and salaries, and we neglect to observe the atmosphere. The cheerfulness of the environment is an important aspect of any job. If you feel you need to have more laughter in your life, then you may have to venture beyond your family and work and seek out friends who laugh.

Think about the changes you'd make if you oriented your life toward people who laugh. When you're interviewing for a new job, look around and see if there's laughter in the workplace. Try to imagine what it would be like to spend most of your life in this atmosphere. If you are single and looking for a partner, listen to the way those prospective men or women laugh. Remember to seek out those people who can laugh.

18. Consider a Teddy Bear

> They stood beneath the window there,
> The King and Mr. Edward Bear,
> And, handsome, if a trifle fat,
> Talked carelessly of this and that . . .
>
> —*A.A. Milne*

I spent a long time hunting for a teddy bear that would help people learn how to hug. I was in Carmel leading a workshop when I wandered into the local toy store and spotted a teddy high on the shelf. After walking around hugging the bear for half an hour to make sure that he was the one, I paid for him and left. I heard a frantic voice from behind calling, "Wait, wait." The woman who had sold me the bear asked, "Please, just one more hug." I knew then that I had a very special bear.

Before I went back to the conference, I stopped to have lunch. I put my bear in the chair next to me. The waitress brought me a menu and, without a word, gave the bear a menu. She put my lunch in front of me and then put a plate in front of the teddy bear. Before long, the other waitresses and customers were aware of us. Pretty soon we were all laughing, and the teddy bear was passed from table to table for hugs.

A square dance was planned that evening at the workshop for recreation. During the rest break, I decided to test the teddy bear. I began to pass the bear around. Everyone wanted to hug the bear, and as they hugged him, their eyes glazed over and beatific smiles passed over their faces. Thirteen-year-old boys were standing in line waiting to hug the bear. It was obvious my bear had passed the test.

I started to take my bear everywhere. He is especially popular in elevators. I was in an elevator in San Francisco one morning when I heard someone behind me say, "And how did Teddy sleep last night?" I turned around and found a gentleman with a briefcase talking to my teddy bear. We had a good laugh and parted company on the next floor.

I had another elevator experience with my teddy bear, whom I named Charlie, when I was in Washington, D.C. I was staying at the Shoreham Hotel and was scheduled to do a presentation for the International Cancer Counselors Association. I stepped into the elevator with Charlie over my arm. I felt a gentle tugging. When I turned, an elegant, obviously foreign gentlemen was shaking the paw of my teddy bear. He was introducing himself and asking the bear what his name was. I said, "Charlie," and the gentleman proceeded to introduce the bear to his friend. We laughed until I reached my floor. I learned later that the two men were members of the World Bank.

Many people have wanted to purchase a bear like mine. When one of my students found a place that would sell to her wholesale, she began to take orders. When she had ten orders, she drove to Los Angeles to pick up the large bears. On the way back she was stopped by a policeman. She had a wonderful time explaining herself and her traveling companions, but, unfortunately, even though the officer laughed, she still got a ticket.

If you're going to walk around with a stuffed bear in your

arms, you're going to raise some eyebrows. If you want, you can tell people that it's for your niece or nephew and let them off the hook. Most won't care who or what it's for if they get to hug it and laugh with you.

19. Risk Looking Foolish

> I call humiliation the universal risk. We take so many risks—even potentially fatal ones—to avoid that.
>
> —*Ralph Keyes*

A friend of mine was late for work one day and inadvertently put on an unmatched pair of shoes. She didn't notice until she was at the office, so there was nothing she could do but suffer through the embarrassment. As it turned out, she had a wonderful day. Instead of trying to hide her feet under her desk, she decided to capitalize on her mistake and use it as a tool for laughter.

If you make a mistake, play with it. Turn it into an opportunity to laugh with yourself, and invite others to laugh along with you.

If you want to go a step further—if you're not afraid of deliberately stepping into the spotlight—then don't wait for a mistake to happen, but wear or carry something outlandish on purpose. I would suggest wearing your everyday clothes and then adding one incongruous touch: a carrot-shaped pen, an arrow through your head, or a teddy bear in your bag.

For several years I participated in the annual University Conference on World Affairs in Boulder, Colorado. It tends to be a serious gathering with serious professional people. During the last conference I attended, I was on a panel about space, the future, and ecosystems. The panel consisted of three members: Carl Hodges of the Biosphere II project; Rusty Schwiekert, astronaut on the Apollo IX mission; and myself, international laugher.

Rusty encouraged me to wear my special hat. It was made up of two party-favor roll-up paper blowers attached to a blow-in tube. Every time a major point was made, he nudged me, and I would blow on the tube, which caused my party favor "horns" to honk and unfurl. I've begun to suspect that I'm assigned to serious panels to help lighten them up.

When I speak to students at the University of California, I occasionally wear an arrow through my head. It keeps me from taking my talk too seriously and absolutely delights the audience. When I talked about this with a workshop group in Dallas, a very elegant woman asked why I would ever wear an arrow through my head. I explained that I really didn't know. At the close of the workshop, when each participant shared what he or she gleaned from the day's experience, this same woman, who turned out to be a vice-president of an elegant department store, announced that she was going to buy herself an arrow to wear to the next board meeting.

Deely Boppers are also useful in promoting laughter. In case you've never seen them, they look like antennae with little pinwheels that spin in the air. You wear them on your head and walk to activate the pinwheels. They make no sense. Put Deely Boppers on your head the next time you're driving in rush-hour traffic. Let them pop up through the sunroof. Watch the smiles and laughs materialize on the other drivers' faces.

For those people who prefer less attention, I'd suggest wearing a funny hat or a pair of Deely Boppers around the house. Wear them while vacuuming, cleaning out the garage, or folding the laundry, and see how they affect your attitude.

20. Have a Pillow Fight

> Comedy is the same as food. You have to have some everyday. It's important for survival, for living on this planet. It's the safety valve that keeps you going. Because the world is partly sane and partly insane. You need perspective. And comedy gives it to you.
>
> —*Sid Caesar*

Pillow fights are a good way to initiate laughter, especially with children. You can hurt a child far worse with a few well-chosen words than you can with a pillow. By matching the intensity of your blows with those of the child you can insure no one gets hurt. I always yell painfully when I get hit so the child feels powerful.

Batacas, which are cloth-covered foam bats, can be used to hit someone harmlessly if the target area is restricted to below the neck. When my sons were teenagers and seemed determined to kill each other, I encouraged them to use batacas. After some earnest hitting, they would invariably end up on the floor, exhausted and laughing. If you want, you can extend this practice to spouses, friends, or work associates.

21. Play Gigglebelly

HUG O' WAR
I will not play at tug o' war.
I'd rather play at hug o' war,
Where everyone hugs
Instead of tugs,
Where everyone giggles
And rolls on the rug,
Where everyone kisses,
And everyone grins,
And everyone cuddles,
And everyone wins.
—*Shel Silverstein*

This game goes by many names, and you might remember playing it when you were younger.

At a gathering of family or friends, have everyone lie on the floor, on his or her back, with each person's head resting upon another person's stomach. It makes for a cozy configuration, although some people might feel uncomfortable with such close contact. But the discomfort is usually temporary, because as soon as one person begins laughing, all of the stomachs and heads in the group start bouncing up and down. To start, the first person says "Ha," the next one "Ha Ha," the third "Ha Ha Ha," and by then the laughter will be rolling.

Since the laughter connection is physical as well as emotional, this is a sure-fire method. In my experience, the only people who are unable to laugh during gigglebelly are those people who have chosen not to play.

22. Appreciate Someone

> The last time I saw Paris,
> her heart was warm and gay,
> I heard the laughter of her heart
> in every street café.
>
> —*Oscar Hammerstein II*

When I tell someone something that I really appreciate about them, they usually laugh and I can laugh along with them.

For whatever reason, our culture is a critical one. We are not accustomed to receiving appreciation, much less giving it.

One of my favorite appreciation stories concerns my son. He was wearing a vibrant green shirt that set off his coloring. The shirt and he were an outstanding combination.

"David, you and that shirt look wonderful together."

He replied that it had a hole in the sleeve.

I repeated, "David, you and that shirt look wonderful together."

"I got it at the rummage sale."

"David, you and that shirt—"

"Yes, I know, we look wonderful together."

We both laughed.

Sometimes it is necessary to be persistent with your appreciation. There are many ways to resist a compliment, but if it gets through, laughter may well ensue.

23. Add the Words "Tee-Hee"

> From the waterfall he named her,
> Minnehaha, Laughing Water.
>
> —*Longfellow*

A middle-aged man stood up in a laughter class and admitted, "I guess I'm a pretty serious person."

"How come?" I asked.

"Well . . . " he said, "Because I'm an engineer."

"That's serious, all right," I agreed.

"Oh, yes." He nodded, restraining an impulse to smile. "Engineering is quite a serious profession."

"Why don't you tell us just *how* serious it is?"

He laughed, embarrassed. "Oh, it's *very* serious," he assured me.

"All right," I said, "then why don't you just tell the group with your most serious face, 'I am a very serious engineer!'"

So he pronounced the words, loud and clear: *"I am a very serious engineer!"* He had to laugh. He couldn't *not* laugh. The simple act of focusing on his seriousness was causing it to dissolve.

"Now tell the group: 'I am a serious engineer . . . tee-hee.'" He couldn't make it through the sentence. Every time he tried, he started laughing. The statement was so incongruous that it wouldn't compute. It fried his carefully engineered circuitry, which was the point of the exercise.

Try this yourself. Add a simple "tee-hee" to whatever you take most seriously.

Tell your husband: "I have an important board meeting this morning . . . tee-hee."

Confess to a friend: "My kids are driving me crazy . . . tee-hee."

Say "Life is terminal . . . tee-hee."

Or "The Pentagon's budget . . . tee-hee."

The "tee-hee" connects the playful aspects of your brain with the intellectual. It allows you to laugh, and then you can see the bigger picture.

Once I worked with a woman who had cerebral palsy. She had little laughter in her life, mainly because of the way people responded to her. I asked her to repeat "I have cerebral palsy . . . tee-hee." Her resulting laughter released an enormous amount of tension and did wonders for her attitude. In addition, laughter helped relax many of her spastic movements and speech.

In the same vein, a physician who was attending my class said that when he was at a social gathering and people learned he was a physician, the atmosphere would suddenly become serious. I suggested to him that he tell people, "I am a silly physician." When he reported back, he said that it had made him laugh, and the person who asked about his profession also laughed, thus relieving the tension around the serious business of medicine.

One of my students wrote the words "tee-hee" across the face of his digital watch in order to lighten up his sense of busyness. There are endless variations on this theme. Write "tee-hee" on a piece of paper and tape it to your steering wheel, the door of your refrigerator, your filing cabinet at work, or the drawer where you keep your underwear. Wherever you need to laugh the most—that's where the "tee-hee" belongs.

24. Form a Serious Anonymous Group

> He who laughs, lasts.
>
> —*Norwegian proverb*

After completing a laughter workshop, I am often asked, "How can we keep our laughter going?" I suggest that people organize a Sunday evening once-a-month group where they meet for one hour with only one rule: that there be absolutely no words and that the only sound allowed is laughter. There are several of these groups meeting monthly around the country, and occasionally I get reports of their continuing excess and success.

25. Create Your Own Laughter Exercise

> Ha-ha can lead to ah-*ha!*
>
> —*Arthur Koestler*

Repeat:
I am creative, tee hee.
Then go for it!

ABOUT THE AUTHOR

Annette Goodheart, Ph.D., is a psychotherapist in private practice in Santa Barbara, California. She has worked with cathartic processes—particularly laughter—since 1970. Dr. Goodheart conducts training intensives for professionals and lectures and leads workshops nationally and internationally. She has been featured on numerous international radio and television programs and is an expert at helping people relearn the art of laughing, without ridicule, about those aspects of their lives that aren't really funny.

Some of Dr. Goodheart's programs include:

- "Loss, Laughter, and Healing," presented to the AIDS, Medicine and Miracles Conference in Boulder, Colorado, the AIDS Update in San Francisco, and at Children's Hospital in Los Angeles.
- "Laugh Your Way to Health," presented to the American Academy of Psychotherapists, the Association for Transpersonal Psychology, Napa State Hospital, Miseracordia Psychiatric Hospital, and the British Columbia Health Association.
- "Laughter and Relationships," presented at Esalen Institute, Dupont, Renaissance International, and Quantum.
- "Laughter Therapy," presented at the University of Nice Psychotherapy Association, the Foundation Soleil in Geneva, and the Torino International Humor Conference.

Annette Goodheart has taught laughter classes at Santa Barbara City College and the University of California at Santa Barbara since 1978. She presents seminars, "You and Your Spiritual Funnybone" and "How to Live and Die Laughing." She holds two masters degrees, one in psychology and one in fine arts, as well as a Ph.D. in psychology. As a California-style ordained minister, she has performed many laughing marriages as well as some very silly sermons.

WHAT OTHERS HAVE SAID ABOUT ANNETTE GOODHEART

The lessons about life that I learned in the last five years from Annette and her many friends, as well as from Albie (my teddy bear), are remarkable and important. Albie and laughter have allowed me to communicate more deeply with more people than I thought possible. If I can play a role in conveying these lessons to our faculty, students, staff, and patients, my tenure as dean of a college of medicine will be satisfying and all sorts of people will be the beneficiaries.

—ALLEN H. NEIMS, M.D., PH.D.
Dean, College of Medicine, University of Florida at Gainsville

I am thrilled that Dr. Goodheart's work is finally in print. I have observed her work, watched her videos, and listened to her tapes—each time I am awed and impressed by her warmth, skill, and effectiveness. Her work is indeed unique and wonderful.

—VIOLET OAKLANDER, PH.D., GESTALT THERAPIST
Author of Windows to our Children

Life is terribly, terribly real and sad. That's part of the story, and it's too easy to believe that's all of the story. Life is also very, very funny. My personal experience in one of Annette's workshops showed me how incredibly talented Dr. Goodheart is in opening people to the vital, spacious, dimension of laughter about our sad problems.

—CHARLES T. TART, PH.D.
Professor of Psychology, University of California

I've known Annette Goodheart for years. And never, not once, have I been in her presence for longer than two minutes before rich, genuine, soul-satisfying laughter erupted. Her mind knows the absurdities of the human condition; her heart knows the healing power of hilarity and nothing—not the most profound sadness, nor the most tormenting trouble—can long withstand the light she brings with her to lift the darkness.

—JANET ROACH
Screenwriter, Academy Award nominee (Prizzi's Honor)

I found Annette Goodheart's presentation on laughter fascinating, entertaining, and informative. She teaches us the physiology and psychology of laughter and underlines its importance in everyday life.

—JAMES F. MASTERSON, M.D.
Director, The Masterson Institute

Annette Goodheart has changed my life and the lives of those around me because of her worldview about painful emotions and how to move them. Annette's theories, which she acts out quite successfully in her practice, can help anyone who is reading this book grow as a human being. The book is an act of love that all should read. May you laugh, cry, rage, or otherwise move your emotions while you read her book.

—PATRICK O'BRIEN, MSW, CSW
Director, New York Region,
Downey Side . . . Families for Youth

In her therapeutic work with clients, Annette Goodheart has developed techniques that have allowed her clients to heal deep emotional wounds and then move on to healthier and happier living. Her unique style of using laughter in her work is a welcome addition to cathartic therapy. In addition, she incorporates this in her own life to handle the many stresses of everyday life. She is upbeat and positive and she laughs a lot. Her warm, contagious laughter often brings a smile to those around her, lightening their spirits as well.

—MARY WATTS CRUTCHFIELD, M.D., P.A.
Psychiatrist, Dallas, Texas

Good Stuff to Buy!

Call, write, e-mail:

Phone:	805-966-0025
Fax:	805-966-6146
E-mail:	**teehee@teehee.com**
Website:	**www.laughtercoach.com** and **www.teehee.com**
Address:	635 Alisos Street, Santa Barbara, CA 93103

CD's & AUDIO CASSETTES

All cd's and cassette tapes can be purchased separately. You can save money purchasing a cassette album. These tapes were recorded live at vario workshops and seminars.

Album1: Laugh Your Way to Health

Includes: Laugh Your Way to Health; Cathartic Laughter: Why It Wor Laughter & Relationships: A Very Serious Business; Loss, Laughter & Tea Sex—Tee Hee.

Laugh Your Way To Health

This is a **double-cassette or CD** (60 minutes each) set which discusses the overall approach to the use of laughter in the healing process. It includes information, group participation, and live demonstrations on the use of laughte with life-threatening diseases and emotional turmoil. These tapes were recorde at the Healing Power of Laughter and Play Conference in San Francisco.

Cathartic Laughter: Why It Works (60 min.)

This recording presents a different approach to the concept of illness and disease. It is an exploration of the process of catharsis: why we laugh, cry, rag etc. and how it affects our bodies and minds. It shows how we can use this knowledge to make our lives more enjoyable, less tension filled, and mentally and physically healthier.

Laughter & Relationships: A very Serious Business (90 min.)

Studies have shown that people who laugh together have more lasting and enjoyable relationships. This recording brings a fresh new approach to understanding and lightening up stressful relationships. It illustrates how laughing together bonds people in a very special way.

Loss, Laughter & Tears (90 min.)
Designed for those who need to cry before they laugh, this recording presents a light approach to releasing the emotions surrounding loss. It is a demonstration of the close relationships between laughter and tears in the mourning-grieving experience. Looking at loss (from major losses to minor ones), this recording explains the roles of laughing and crying in the healing process.

Sex—Tee Hee (90 min.) Is sex too serious for you? Do you suffer from guilt, fear, boredom? Is the excitement gone? Here is a look at the role of laughter in our sexual relationships, illustrating how seriously we take sex, the need to make sex more fun, and the use of laughter as an additional tension reliever—when all else fails!

Loss, Laughter & Healing (60 min.) This audio recording illustrates the connection between laughter and tears by addressing the belief system that surrounds both. Feel free to join in with the laughter and tears contained in this recording.

Laugh Track (60min.) Dr. Steve Allen, Jr., joins Dr. Goodheart in this "All Laughter, No Lecture" recording.

VIDEO CASSETTES

Laughter At The Mall (20 min.)

This video is all laughter. For a free book and red nose, people of all shapes, ages, colors & sizes volunteered to laugh for the camera (with some minor laughter coaching from Dr. Goodheart). Someone on this tape is bound to make you laugh!

Laugh Your Way to Health (60 min.) ABC-CLIO *Video Library Review* gives this tape four stars! "This hour long video is a witty presentation filled with practical information. Goodheart spends a major portion of the program practicing what she preaches—laughter. She is an excellent teacher."

The Art of Laughter Therapy (105 min.)
Dr. Goodheart demonstrates the techniques of laughter therapy with four volunteers, chosen randomly from the audience, who have personal issues they need to laugh about. These personal issues include codependency, being too intense, worrying, and being a father. Between each demonstration the audience raises numerous questions fro discussion pertaining to personal and professional topics.

Laughter for Loving, 1 & 2 (70 min.)
Both videos start with a brief lecture by Dr. Goodheart and consist of a mini therapy session with three different couples presenting various "serious problems. These videos are a gentle and fun reminder of how important it is to lighten up our "serious" relationships so we can get back to enjoying each other's company.

"Red Noses"
Light and comfortable, these sponge noses fit every shape and size!

"Charlie Bear"
Dr. Goodheart presents most of her lectures and workshops with her traveling companion, Charlie Bear, especially made for her by Charm Corp. He is a lovable squeezable, 27-inch stuffed animal, especially useful for helping people relearn the art of hugging. "Charlie's an expensive bear", she adds, "but he's a very cheep relationship."

THIS BOOK

Laughter Therapy, How to Laugh About Everything in Your Life That Isn't Really Funny.

Other Good Stuff

Dr. Goodheart offers a variety of programs for groups and individuals:

- Speeches and workshops for profit and nonprofit organizations
- Professional and in-service trainings for individuals and groups
- Intensive therapy for individuals, couples, relationships, families, and small notions
- Consultations and supervision for professionals
- Weddings and sermons
- Laughter Coaching

Speeches and Workshops

Speeches vary in length from three minutes (all laughter, no words) to two hours. The ideal length of time is one and a half hours in a cool environment (laughter heats up a room by ten degrees). By this time most folks need to drain their tanks.

Speeches are given to all sorts of groups: corporations, conferences, businesses, churches, public agencies, conventions, schools, universities, hospitals, etc. Laughter content can be adapted to any group and its special needs. Groups have varied in size from ten to 3,800.

Some selected titles have been "Plerking: The Perks of Putting Laughter and Play to Work," "Laugh Your Way to Health," "How to Live & Die Laughing," "Sex—Tee Hee," "Loss, Laughter & Healing," "Laughter & Learning in the Classroom," "The Laughter Connection," and "Laughter & The Lightness of Embarrassment: Charlie Chaplin's Contribution to Cultural Catharsis" (presented at the Sorbonne, Paris, 1989).

Workshops range in length from one and a half hours to many days. Often, after presenting a keynote address at a conference, it will be followed by a workshop. Before- and after-conference workshops (often called institutes) can be scheduled. All workshops contain some lecture, discussion, question-and-answer period, demonstrations, and lots of laughter.

Almost every year in the spring and fall (sometimes in the winter), Dr. Goodheart holds a public one-day workshop in Santa Barbara. These are intermittent, and dates and costs can be obtained by phone, fax, or "on-line." Costs of speeches and workshops for other groups can be negotiated by the same methods.

Professional Training Program

Dr. Goodheart holds a seven-day professional training each August in beautiful Santa Barbara, California. This week-long laughter event is *not* about humor. By recognizing the difference between laughter and humor, one discovers the key to understanding the healing power of cathartic laughter.

This yearly event attracts trainees from all over the world from professions as varied as therapists, ministers, nurses, humor specialists, teachers, social workers, physicians, and anyone who will apply her laughter techniques in the workplace.

The number of participants is limited to the size of Dr. Goodheart's living room (up to twenty-four). In this relaxed environment you will have an opportunity to:

- Learn to contact the laughter within: experience an easier time connecting with your patients/clients in a caring way
- Increase your ability to take risks, have fun, enjoy yourself
- Address your own cathartic processes
- Help break down old patterns of rigid thinking and being
- Improve access to your own intelligence and creativity
- Increase your sense of physical well being

As well as addressing the personal needs of the participants, this Laughter Training Program provides *practical tools* to help professionals to:

- Facilitate emotional movement in clients/patients
- Develop skills to assist clients/patients discover how to play with their stress, tension, and pain
- Learn about the "dark side" of laughter: the negative effects of ridicule, teasing, joke telling, tickling
- Design and implement effective "laughter groups"
- Increase your enjoyment and effectiveness working with clients/patients dealing with issues surrounding cancer, AIDS, incest, depression, divorce, death

The Laughter Therapy Training program offers a unique balance of lectures, discussion, participatory sessions, case discussions, practice sessions, and critiques. Time is set aside for participants to "digest" their new learning, as well as to avail themselves of Santa Barbara's charms.

All participants receive a course manual/study guide packed with reference materials highlighting the role of laughter and the other cathartic processes in reducing stress, controlling pain, and family therapy. In addition, "playful tools" are provided for practitioners to use in their work, for both professional and personal enjoyment.

Unique video practicums allow participants to have their own in-session participatory work taped for future reference. Of special interest to therapists and critical-care counselors are the live demonstrations of actual sessions between Dr. Goodheart and patients with AIDS or cancer and incest survivors.

CEU credits are available for nurses.

An advanced training is available for all graduates once a year on Presidents' Day Weekend in February. For the date and cost of the next Laughter Training, write, call, fax, or go "on-line."

Annette Goodheart, Ph.D.
635 N. Alisos Street, Santa Barbara, CA 93103

Phone	(805) 966-0025
Fax	(805) 966-6146*
Home Page	www.teehee.com
E-Mail	teehee@teehee.com

In-Service Trainings

Dr. Goodheart is often called in to teach healthy laughter techniques to businesses, corporations, public agencies, hospitals or other administrative staffs.

These techniques produce a freer workplace where ridicule and put-downs (including sexual harassment) can be replaced with laughter that is non-hurtful, healthy, and connecting. As a result, the interaction of lightness and laughter produces more creativity, less stress-related illness, and less turnover.

Intensive Therapy

In addition to private hourly therapy sessions, Dr. Goodheart offers the opportunity for an intensive therapy experience. These "intensives" can be a regular monthly event (often for people who drive in from other cities) or a one-shot, once-a-year occasion.

Intensives involve a condensed number of sessions lasting from three hours to six days. The most hours per day has been ten, and the most hours per week (five days) has been thirty-five hours. All intensives can be negotiated as to number of days and hours per day. The cost is the same as for one hour of regular therapy. Intensives can be obtained for couples, relationships, siblings, and friends as well as for individuals.

*If this doesn't work the first time, try again—the cat sits on the warm machine and changes it!

Many clients have found this form of therapy to be a boost that complements their ongoing work. Their therapist's permission is required. For those not in therapy, but who are "stuck" or generally dissatisfied, an intensive can be a wonderful cathartic boost out of the doldrums. If this kind of therapy interests you, please call for further information. Dr. Goodheart is available for phone follow-up.

Consultations & Supervision for Professionals

Consultation and supervision can be done in person or by phone. Dr. Goodheart does weekly supervision for professionals from many backgrounds and for graduate trainees who need special guidance in using laughter techniques.

Weddings and Sermons

Dr. Goodheart has performed many laughing weddings for persons who want to start their lives together with a light touch. Many have written marriage pledges to one another to keep laughing through the tough parts. (One occasion on the beach was attended by thirty dolphins!) As an ordained minister, Dr. Goodheart can perform these ceremonies, and they are even seriously legal.

Many denominations and spiritual groups have requested a "Laughter Sermon." Dr. Goodheart has become somewhat famous for what she refers to as her "Silly Sermons." These presentations are usually thirty minutes long and can be repeated for a second service. Often this sermon is followed or preceded by a workshop for the congregation and sometimes includes the general public.

Random Reading

Allen, Steve. *How to be Funny*. New York: McGraw-Hill, 1987.

Casriel, Daniel. *A Scream Away from Happiness*. New York: Grossett and Dunlap, 1972.

Chapman, A.J., and Foote, H.C. (eds.) *Humor and Laughter: Theory, Research, and Application*. London: John Wiley & Sons, 1976.

Churchill, James S., and Grene, Marjorie. *Laughing and Crying*. Evanston, Indiana: Northwestern University Press, 1979.

Cousins, Norman. *Anatomy of an Illness as Perceived by the Patient*. New York: Norton, 1979.

—. *Head First: The Biology of Hope*. New York: Dutton, 1989.

Diamond, John. *Your Body Doesn't Lie*. New York: Harper & Row, 1979.

Eastman, Max. *Enjoyment of Laughter*. New York: Simon & Schuster, 1936.

Freud, Sigmund. *Jokes and Their Relationship to the Unconscious*. New York: Norton, 1905.

Jackins, Harvey. *The Human Side of Human Beings*. Seattle: Rational Island Publishers, 1974.

Koestler, Arthur. *The Act of Creation*. New York: Macmillan, 1964.

Kubie, Lawrence S. "The destructive potential of humor in psychotherapy." *American Journal of Psychiatry* 127 (1971): 861-66.

Long, James W. *The Essential Guide to Prescription Drugs*. HarperCollins, 1991.

Miller, Alice. *For Your Own Good: Hidden Cruelty in Child Rearing and the Roots of Violence*. New York: Farrar, Straus, Geroix, 1983.

Moody, Raymond A., Jr. *Laugh After Laugh*. Jacksonville, Florida: Headwaters Press, 1978.

Naisbitt, John. *Taking Laughter Seriously*. Albany, New York: State University of New York Press, 1983.

Pelletier, K.R. *Mind as Healer, Mind as Slayer*. Delta Books, 1977.

Robinson, Vera M. *Humor and the Health Professions: The Therapeutic Use of Humor in Health Care*. Thorofare, New Jersey: Slack, 1991.

Scheff, Thomas J. *Catharsis in Healing, Ritual, and Drama*. Berkeley: University of California Press, 1979.

Siegel, Bernie. *Love, Medicine, and Miracles.* San Francisco: Harper & Row, 1989.

Simonton, O. Carl, et al. *Getting Well Again.* Los Angeles: J.P. Tarcher, Inc., 1978.

Stearns, Fredrich R. *Laughing: Physiology, Pathology, Psychology, Pathopsychology, and Development.* Springfield, Illinois: Charles C. Thomas, 1972.

Ward, Milton. *The Brilliant Function of Pain.* New York: Optimus Books, 1979.

Weinstein, Matt, and Goodman, Joel. "Playfair." *In Context* 13 (spring 1986): 14-16.

Wolfe, Sidney M., M.D., and Hope, Rose-Ellen, R.Ph. *Worst Pills, Best Pills, II.* The Public Citizen Research Group, 1993.

Ziv, Avner. *Personality and Sense of Humor.* New York: Springer, 1984.